MODERN SPORTING GUNS

MODERN
SPORTING GUNS

CHRISTOPHER AUSTYN

· THE ·
SPORTSMAN'S
PRESS
LONDON

Published by The Sportsman's Press 1994

To
C.E.B.
and My Parents

Distributed in the USA by Safari Press Inc
P.O. Box 3095, Long Beach, CA 90803

A catalogue record for this book
is available from the British Library

ISBN 0-948253-60-6

Printed in Great Britain by
BAS Printers Limited, Over Wallop, Hampshire

CONTENTS

ACKNOWLEDGEMENTS

My thanks are due to the Photographic Department of Christie's, including Ryszard Durka and James Barclay-Brown and Natasha Hanscomb (who typed the manuscript).

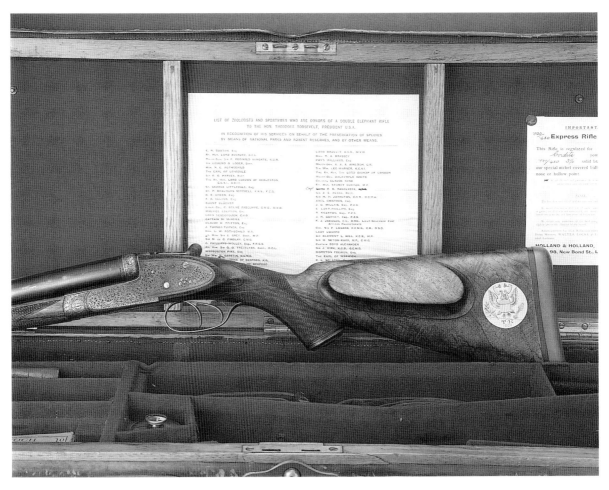

President Theodore Roosevelt's .500/.450 'Royal' sidelock non-ejector rifle, No. 19109. This rifle was presented to the President in 1909 by the leading statesmen, sportsmen and clergy of England and the dedication in the case lid includes, amongst others, the names of F.C. Selous, C. Phillipps-Wolley, Abel Chapman and J.G. Millais. This rifle was the most powerful Roosevelt ever owned and used and is a fitting accompaniment to one of the President's most famous quips: 'Walk softly and carry a big stick'.
(Photo: R.L. Wilson)

LIST OF COLOUR PLATES

17 A .240 (Flanged) 'Royal' double-barrelled sidelock ejector rifle by Holland & Holland, and a .375 (H & H Belted Rimless Magnum) double-barrelled boxlock ejector rifle by W.J. Jeffery.

18 A .458 (Winchester Magnum) 'Royal' double-barrelled sidelock ejector rifle by Holland & Holland.

19 A fine .375 Magnum (Flanged) 'Royal' double-barrelled sidelock ejector rifle.

20 A .458 (Winchester Magnum) 'Royal' double-barrelled sidelock ejector rifle by Holland & Holland and a .400/.360 ($2\frac{3}{4}$ in.) double-barrelled boxlock non-ejector rifle by W. Evans.

21 A .250 double-barrelled boxlock ejector rifle by J. Rigby.

22 Two good examples of increasingly rare pistols, a .577 double-barrelled hammer Howdah pistol by Army & Navy and a .410 double-barrelled sidelock ejector pistol by L. Douard (Tours).

23 An unusual Asprey's silver place finder and a silver 'Patent Pathfinder' by G. White & Co. The engraved and gold-washed lock work of a Holland & Holland sidelock.

24 A fine Eley 'Sporting amd Military' cartridge board.

INTRODUCTION

This book is intended for those new to the gun business. When I joined the Sporting Gun Department, some thirteen years ago, I know that I found it difficult to find books that gave a broad approach to the subject and I have always felt that a profusely illustrated text was vital. I hope my readers will find this book both sufficiently broad in scope and interestingly illustrated; the next step to a fuller understanding will be the actual handling of the guns themselves.

A rare Dickson patent side-opening over-and-under 12-bore gun by J. Dickson, No. 7540. The gun was completed in 1952.

Only twelve guns are believed to have been built on this system (nine 12-bores and three 20-bores) which is based on Dickson's famous round-action. In this fascinating adaptation, the gun is turned on its side and the bar is reduced in depth. One of the consequences of this design is that, as the barrels are not mounted centrally in the action, the assessment of cast is difficult. The gun brought 6500 gns at Christie's in 1975 and is worth many times that today.

I

Best English Guns

What is a 'best' English gun? The basic configuration is more or less standard, although it is in the nature of a best gun for it to have any number of additional refinements and peculiarities as they are all built to individual specifications. The standard 12-bore configuration is a side-by-side double-barrelled sidelock ejector gun, weighing something in the region of $6\frac{1}{2}$ to $6\frac{3}{4}$ lb and with a barrel length of anything between 25 and 30 in., and most commonly 28 to 30 in. Stock lengths, of course, vary enormously, for obvious reasons but an average stock length of about $14\frac{3}{4}$ in. is ideal. Shorter stocks are less popular and extreme shortness will sometimes necessitate restocking. Over the last ten years, the ideal barrel length has proved to be 28 in., with a slightly reduced popularity for 30 in. barrels and there has been a general movement towards $2\frac{3}{4}$ in. chambers, largely because of the strengths of the United States and European markets and the growing accessibility of shooting abroad. Chokes, of course, are a matter of taste, but the ideal seems to be about $\frac{1}{4}$ and $\frac{1}{2}$ for normal game shooting.

The specifications I have outlined above are more or less standard, but they will vary enormously. A collector will be confronted with lightweight guns, 'pigeon' guns with added weight, guns with very little choke or very tight choke, and so on. But if he were to come to this market with little or no experience, how would he identify a gun of this type? In my experience, most people will understand those factors which directly affect the use of a gun, but they are generally less certain of the type and this applies just as much to people who have owned a gun for a long time, perhaps inheriting it from a father or grandfather. As we have seen, a best gun is most commonly a side-by-side sidelock

Holland & Holland 12-bore (2 in.) single trigger 'Royal Twelve-Two Self-Opener' sidelock ejector gun No. 33021, built in 1934. Note the characteristic 'hand-detachable' lever and the bold foliate-scroll engraving – the dominant Holland & Holland engraving motif in their classic game guns.

The self-opening compressor on the underside of the barrels of a Holland & Holland 'Royal' sidelock ejector gun.

ejector gun; there are two major exceptions to this rule which we shall come to later. The sidelock is easily identifiable, although I have probably spent more time on the telephone attempting to describe such guns to an unwitting owner than I have in selling them. A sidelock will have two separate lockplates set into the 'head' of the stock where it joins the action body, and each lockplate will carry its own independent firing mechanism. The overall shape of the lockplate will vary from maker to maker but the basic shape is always the same. Guns by Rigby's and older Holland & Holland 'Royals' have perhaps the most distinctive variation with a dipped edge on the upper side of the lockplate. Other makers will give the lockplate slight differences in width and in the shaping of the 'tail' where it can become more pointed or rounded. Sidelocks by Atkin and Lang, for example, generally have narrower and more pointed lockplates and the same will quite often be the case with the 'Imperial' grade guns by Harrison & Hussey, Lang and Hussey and Hussey & Hussey. Lockplates by Purdey, Holland & Holland, Boss and Woodward are generally of the classic broad and rounded shape.

Sidelock mechanisms fall into two general types: back-action mechanisms in which the mainspring is situated to the rear of the lockplate, behind the action body; and bar-action mechanisms whereby the mainspring lies along the bar of the action. Most sidelocks are built on the latter principle, back-action locks being reserved, in the main, for double rifles in which, because of the need for added strength, less of the action bar is machined away. In either case, the outer surface of the lockplate bears several circular pins which serve to locate the lockwork on the inner side and which show, therefore, the positions of the mainspring peg, the tumbler pivot, the sear and interceptor pivots, and the bridle, which acts as the framework for the entire assembly; because these pins locate the mechanism it is possible, therefore, to identify which type of lockwork a sidelock has. A bar-action sidelock will have a pin at the extreme forward end of the lockplate (the mainspring peg); this will be absent in a back-action mechanism. There is an exception to all this which can be confusing. Some makers, notably Churchill's and, sometimes, Purdey and Holland & Holland, made 'pinless lockplates' in which the pins do not intrude on the surface of the lockplate. The idea was to keep the lockplate free of intrusions to allow for unbroken engraving, and with today's growth in fine 'game' engraving, such guns are more and more commonly encountered.

A point of interest is that the tumbler pivot or axle, around which the tumbler rotates on firing or cocking, also runs through the lockplate to its outer surface and as it also rotates on firing or cocking, some makers mark it with an indicator or 'tell-tale' – usually a gold-inlaid line or a small arrow – which will show, therefore, whether the gun is cocked or not. In Woodward sidelocks and older Holland & Holland 'Royals' this tumbler pivot will protrude quite markedly above the surface of the lockplate.

An ejector system is just about standard for any type of gun today but it is possible to find a number of guns built without ejectors. These, for obvious reasons, will normally date from the last two decades of the nineteenth century and will be 'transitional' guns in the sense that they provide a link between hammer guns, in which ejectors are rare, and the later fully-fledged hammerless guns

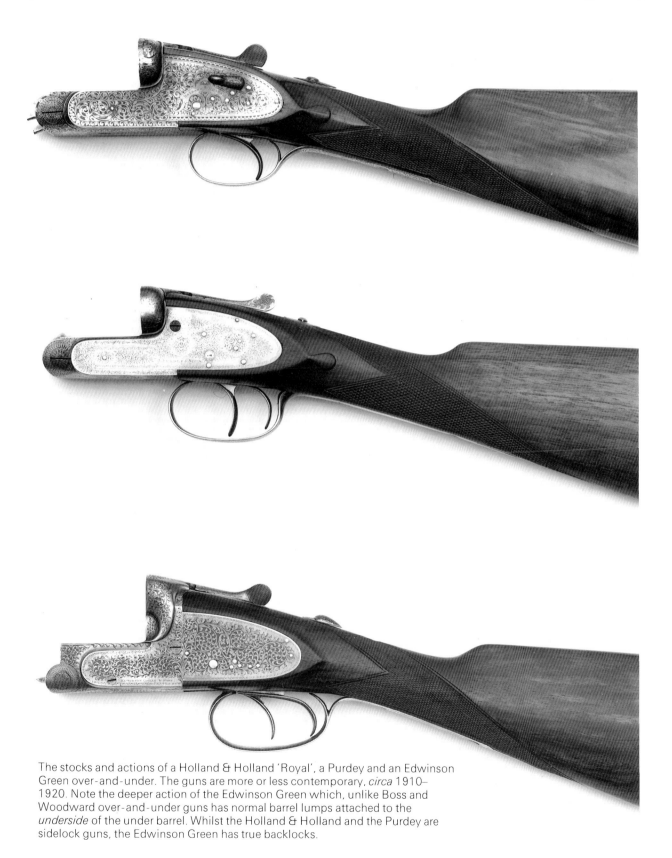

The stocks and actions of a Holland & Holland 'Royal', a Purdey and an Edwinson Green over-and-under. The guns are more or less contemporary, *circa* 1910–1920. Note the deeper action of the Edwinson Green which, unlike Boss and Woodward over-and-under guns has normal barrel lumps attached to the *underside* of the under barrel. Whilst the Holland & Holland and the Purdey are sidelock guns, the Edwinson Green has true backlocks.

of which they are almost always a feature. An examination of the extractors at the breech-ends of the barrels will show quite clearly whether a gun has ejectors or not. If the extractor is built in one piece, the gun does not have ejectors; the extractor is simply cammed forward by the extractor cam on the knuckle of the action to enable the spent cases to be pulled manually from the gun. Primary extraction, in which the extractors are pushed forward slightly is also a part of ejector systems and an ejector system is clearly fitted to the gun if the extractor is in two pieces, with each section working independently.

The purpose of ejectors is quite simply to facilitate the more rapid loading and unloading of the gun; non-ejector guns became restricted to very specialized forms of shooting – training for beginners, for example, and wildfowling with large bore guns. This is not to say that non-ejector guns are boring or of low quality. Some are, but it is possible to encounter best guns without ejectors but with just about every other refinement – these are normally the domain of collectors and 'occasional' sportsmen, or they will be converted to ejector.

The two most commonly encountered ejector systems are the Southgate and Deeley patents. There are others, of course, just as there are numerous patents for just about every other feature of a classic sporting gun. There is no question about which is the most popular. The Southgate is easier to regulate and is generally simpler in construction and shooting men and collectors should familiarize themselves with the identification of the two patents. The ejector kickers in the Southgate system are much closer to the end of the forend iron and the tumbler peg, around which they rotate, will be seen just below them. The kickers are further back in the Deeley and there is no tumbler peg as this system is contained in its own 'box' further back in the forend iron.

We now have an explanation of the term 'sidelock ejector'. Guns of this type

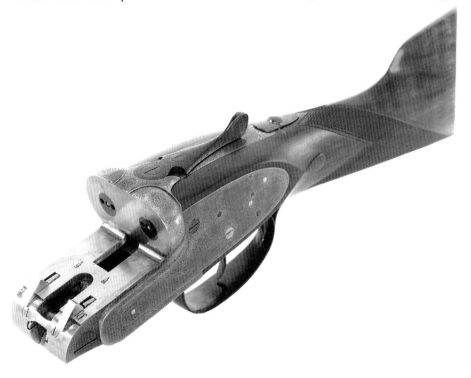

A classic Purdey sidelock ejector gun. The self-opening 'kickers' or compressors are clearly visible above the 'knuckle' of the action as are the disc-set strikers and the clearly impressed London 'view' proof marks.

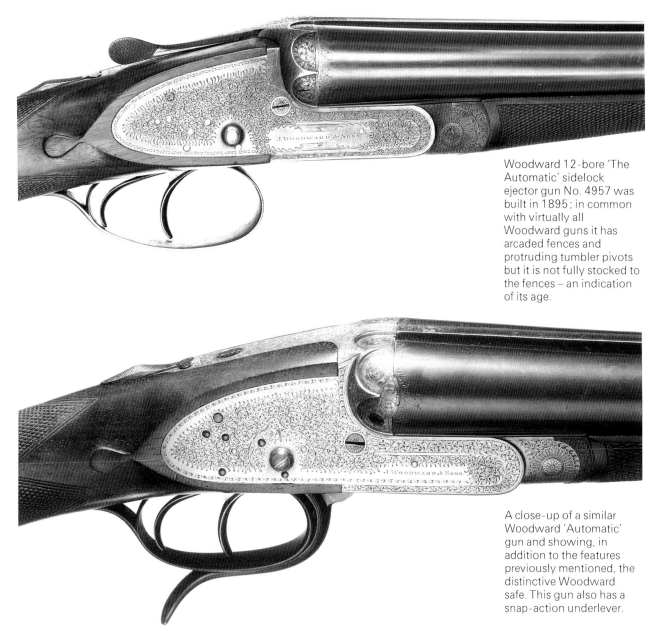

Woodward 12-bore 'The Automatic' sidelock ejector gun No. 4957 was built in 1895; in common with virtually all Woodward guns it has arcaded fences and protruding tumbler pivots but it is not fully stocked to the fences – an indication of its age.

A close-up of a similar Woodward 'Automatic' gun and showing, in addition to the features previously mentioned, the distinctive Woodward safe. This gun also has a snap-action underlever.

have a number of added features, some of which will be common to other types of guns. The first of these features will concern themselves with the opening of the gun and with the bolting of the barrels to the action body. Both of the features normally used to effect these have become classics of design. The first is the Scott spindle which is linked to a toplever in order to facilitate opening, and the second is the Purdey bolt which serves to secure the barrels to the action by means of a bolt sliding in the bar of the action. There are exceptions to the first feature, but none, nowadays, to the second, and the reason for this is quite simple. The first has a direct affect upon the actual handling of the gun in use and some people found that they preferred sidelevers and underlevers to the toplever. In the second instance, the actual bolting of the barrels is a pure

(*This page and opposite*)
A comparison of action
shapes

Woodward *circa* 1901

Boss Round-Body *circa*
1900

Purdey *circa* 1897

Purdey *circa* 1894

Grant *circa* 1887

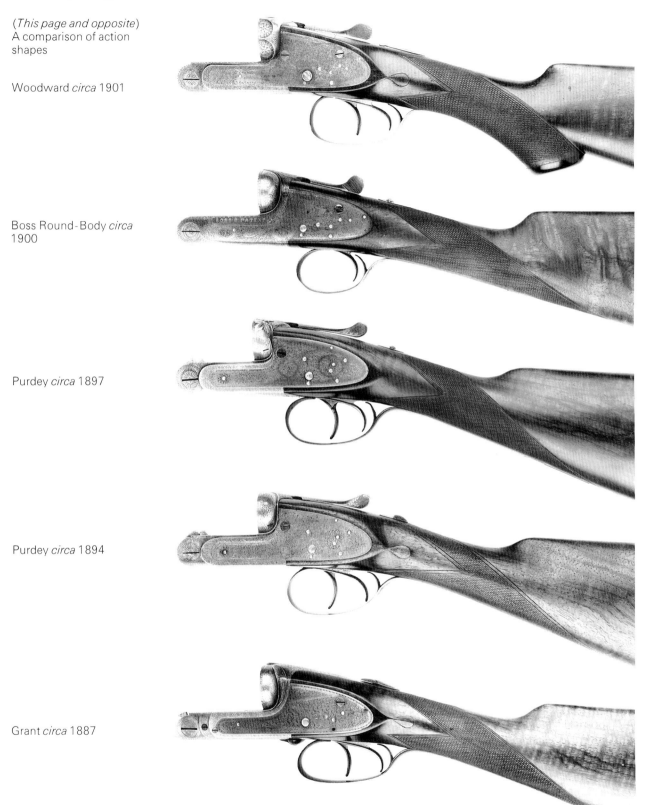

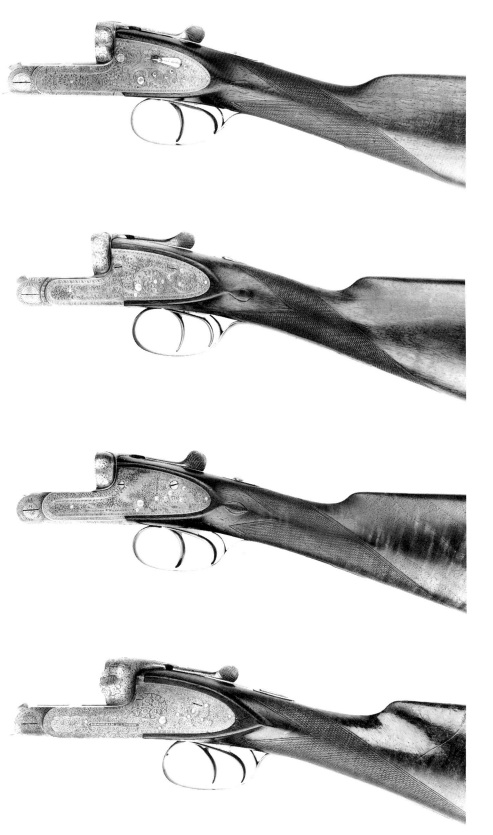

Holland & Holland 'Royal'
circa 1908

Churchill 'Imperial XXV'
circa 1933

Holland & Holland 'No. 2
Grade' *circa* 1899

de luxe pigeon gun by C.
Hunt *circa* 1910–1920.

The underside of Boss 12-bore round body single trigger self-opening sidelock ejector gun No. 8600, built in 1938. This illustration shows the distinctive 'round-body' shaping of the sides and underside of the action body; the elegance of this design makes these guns particularly sought after.

mechanical feature and it can be linked to just about any type of lever. We find, therefore, that makers such as Grants and Boss produced a good number of sidelever guns, whilst Woodwards constructed 'Automatic' guns built on snap-action underlevers.

The features so far discussed are largely concerned with the actions of best guns. The action or action body itself starts life as a solid and somewhat unprepossessing lump of steel, but it is ultimately the receptacle for all the intricate lockwork and bolting and opening mechanisms. The steel used in its construction should be strong and elastic as it will have to endure flexing pressures as the gun is fired, particularly at the junction between the breech face and the action bar. The 'actioning' of a best gun is, therefore, the most time-consuming and expensive part of the gun-making procedure. The lockwork was, and still is in most cases, bought ready made-up, albeit crudely and requiring extensive finishing, from specialist 'lock filers' and the names of Brazier's and Chilton's who built the majority of the locks of best English guns, remain famous today. The one major exception to this nowadays is Holland & Holland, who make most of their own.

Also associated with the action body is the 'furniture', a term which refers, in the main, to the triggerguard and top and bottom straps. Situated on the top strap, just short of the toplever will be the safe. In all guns this normal top-safe will act to bolt the trigger blades, preventing them from being raised should the triggers be accidentally pulled. The majority of safes are automatic, that is, returning automatically to safe on the opening of the toplever, but some are manual, thereby requiring the firer to switch back to 'safe' after the firing of the gun. In most best guns, however, there will also be an intercepting safe within the lockwork which acts to intercept a falling tumbler should a mishap occur with the mechanism. This is, of course, an extremely unlikely occurrence but there is always the possibility of the point at which the tumbler-sear catches in its 'bent' becoming worn or being subjected to a sharp jolt. An intercepting safe is therefore a second form of insurance, and because it provides a physical block between the tumbler and striker it is deemed to be of considerable importance.

A good percentage of best sidelock actions also have striker discs. These are circular inserts in the standing breech, or, in Purdey terminology, the 'detonating', through which the strikers project upon firing. They are found where the strikers are fitted from the front and they can be renewed if the face of the standing breech becomes pitted or corroded. They are also sometimes used as a form of 'gas check' – a method of releasing abnormal pressures or gas emissions away from the point of detonation. Where this is the case, the safety channel runs from the striker disc, through the standing breech to a small pin on its outer edge; examination of this pin will reveal a small hole or vent concealed in the slot. Gas checks will also sometimes be found as simple channels cut into the face of the standing breech, connecting the striker with the outer edge; this is particularly the case with older Holland & Holland 'Royals'.

The barrels of best guns are normally constructed in two main ways: with chopper lumps or with dovetail lumps. Occasionally they can also be constructed with 'through' lumps but this is less commonly encountered. Whereas the two other methods are often applied to hammer guns, the chopper lump method came into being as a result of the introduction of the use of steel for barrels which enabled the tube and lump to be forged as one piece. The chopper lump is therefore an integral part of each barrel, both parts being brazed together on the joining of the tubes, and they can be identified by the line or joint running along the lumps. This is not always apparent, particularly where the lumps are worn or marked, but it can usually be seen between the lumps. It is clear that as integral parts of the barrel, chopper lumps are the strongest and safest method of securing the barrels, but they are also the most expensive. Dovetail lumps are built separately and then fitted between the barrels, the strength being supplied by the mechanical joint and by the brazing which secures the lumps in position. There are, of course, other methods of joining the barrels but unless the gun has been rebarrelled to a lower standard, they will not normally be found on best guns. The next chapter will discuss these methods as they are most commonly found in boxlocks. Purdey guns are invariably built with chopper lumps, but it is common to find Boss, Holland & Holland and Woodward guns with dovetail lumps. Other makers would have used either method in their best guns, presumably according to the financial restrictions of their customers. The only potential drawback with dovetailed lumps is that it is sometimes possible for them to work loose. Through lumps are identified quite easily because they extend between the barrels as far as the top rib, thereby creating a very strong joint.

An early 12-bore 'Royal' sidelock ejector gun by Holland & Holland, No. 14117. Note the dipped edge to the lock plate – an indication of its age – and the protruding tumbler pivot, another characteristic of this early style. The gun dates from the turn of the century.

All the materials used in a best gun will be of the very highest quality. Before the advent of the use of steel in barrels, a best gun would have been made with Damascus barrels. These are instantly recognizable by the beautiful patterning in the metal; they were made by twisting iron and steel strips together, welding them, and then flattening them into a ribbon which was coiled around a mandril; the ribbon was then welded and forged into a solid tube ready for boring and filing. Finally, the patterning in the metal was accentuated by a process of controlled rusting known as browning. Sometimes the barrels would be etched –

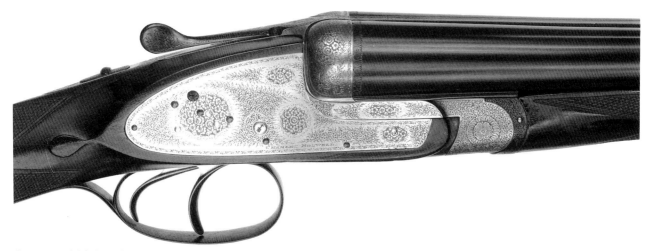

An unusual 16-bore bar-
in-wood sidelock ejector
gun by C. Boswell,
No. 17356; the addition of
a bar-in-wood on a
hammerless gun is most
unusual and is confined, in
general, to hammer guns.

the acid affecting the steel and iron at different rates so that the difference became
even more pronounced. Needless to say, the construction of best grade Damascus
was a very skilled process but the advent of an appropriate steel for use in barrel-
making eliminated the one thing to which the Damascus-making process was
most susceptible – flaws in the substance of the metal itself. The method of
construction of, for example, Sir Joseph Whitworth's 'Fluid Compressed Steel'
in which pressure was applied to the metal as it cooled, effectively eliminated
air pockets and impurities in the metal; with steel, barrels could be made
stronger, lighter and more elastic. Many best guns will be found with the inscription 'Made of Sir Joseph Whitworth's Fluid Compressed Steel' on the top rib
and with the Whitworth trademark of a sheaf of corn stamped on the underside
of the tubes; Purdey and Woodward guns were almost invariably built with
Whitworth steel, but occasionally guns may be found with Vickers, Krupp or
Siemens stamps on the barrels.

The wood used for the stocking of a best gun is walnut and it is generally
reckoned that the best figured wood comes from the junction between the trunk
and root. Blanks taken from further up the trunk will have a straighter and
less interesting figure. The stocking can have a dramatic effect upon the saleability of a gun and there is now a greater appreciation of this than ever before.
In the past it seems to have been largely a matter of luck as to whether a gun
was given a well-figured stock. Purdey guns built in the twenties and thirties,
for example, will often have indifferently-figured stocks – perhaps they were
just less concerned about the appearance of the wood. Boss and Woodward guns
from the same period, on the other hand, are far more likely to have highly-
figured stocks and there is a story, though it might be apocryphal, that Woodward's were given first choice in the selection of new supplies of blanks, closely
followed by Boss and then, sadly, Purdey's. It seems now to be a prerequisite
in the ordering of a new gun that it should have highly-figured wood. The best
walnut has traditionally come from France, but as the supplies of well-figured
wood have diminished, other areas have been explored – wood can now come
from Australia, Turkey, Iran, America and Yugoslavia, each type having its

peculiarities of grain and figure. Much American walnut, for example, tends to be rather scaly in appearance and is reckoned to be more difficult to work. Whatever the origin of the wood, it is important that it satisfies certain basic requirements and walnut has proved itself to be the most reliable wood for stocks because it is good to handle and can be cut and shaped well. It is also strong and flexible. As with the steel used in the barrels, which will expand slightly as the charge passes up the bore, so with the stock which flexes at the 'hand' when the gun is used. Walnut is also largely resistant to splitting and it is a comparatively light wood – another important consideration when building guns to a specific weight. Stock blanks require anything up to ten years for seasoning and there is considerable skill in judging a piece of wood – the figure can change as the stocker works further into the wood, and it can sometimes contain knots and 'shakes' which can make it virtually useless. In the case of the Greener 'St George' gun, for example, which will be discussed in greater detail in the next chapter, a remarkable piece of wood was saved for posterity by the careful filling in of a large number of natural holes in the stock.

There are two major finishes that will be given to the stock on a best gun – an English 'oil' finish which I find generally more attractive, or a highly-polished 'French' finish. A good oil finish accentuates the figure in the wood more fully – a very high shine, naturally, tends to obscure it; the shaping and fitting of the wood requires considerable wood-working skills. Certain makers have particular stylistic differences in the way stocks are shaped and chequered. In most guns, the 'hand' of the stock will be almost circular in section, but Holland & Holland give their stocks a diamond section at this point – which is designed to stop the stock turning in the hand. Chequering prevents the hand slipping on the wood, but it is also a decorative feature and will be cut with an average density of 20 to 24 lines to the inch. The borders of the chequering will also sometimes be given a more ornate finish, and there are examples of unchequered

A 12-bore sidelock ejector gun by W. & C. Scott, No. 55673. The gun is probably a late model 'Monte Carlo B' and features de luxe engraving of the type occasionally found on guns built in the early years of the century. The oak leaf is a common engraving motif on best guns; the ducks are touchingly naive in their representation and form a sharp contrast to modern day gun engraving with its emphasis upon detailed realism.

A classic decorative motif used by a number of English makers is the acanthus leaf. In this instance, a Purdey 12-bore sidelock ejector gun, the fences are carved, but it was also customary to relief-engrave the fences in a similar fashion. Note also the short, positive Purdey safe with its raised and chequered 'bead'.

stocks – Greener, for example, eschewed chequering on his 'Rational' stocks and some Dickson and MacNaughton guns do not have chequering.

The forend of a best gun, or the part that joins the barrels and action, assists in cocking the tumblers and houses the ejector system, will normally be elegant and slender in form and it will be bolted to the forend-loop on the barrels. The modern method of bolting the forend is the result of considerable past experimentation; it is known as the Anson bolt and consists of a bolt activated by a small press catch in the tip of the forend. The other method sometimes encountered is the Deeley system in which a loop situated in the body of the forend is raised to free the catch.

An expert finish is vital to the appearance of a best gun; it is, after all, literally what you see of the gun. Some people will be overawed by a flashily-engraved gun and will not, for example, take time to inspect the fit of the lockplates or the shaping of the wood to the action and furniture. Needless to say, these things should be just about perfect in a best gun, but they can be overlooked. So what should their characteristics be in a best gun? When considering finish, we are led naturally to the engraving of a gun and whilst I will devote more attention to this further on, we should examine the general styles. There are two classic styles of English engraving and some other variations. The first, and most traditional, is what Purdey's call their 'standard fine', an understated arrangement of bouquets and scrolls. These are executed on a more or less unvarying pattern on Purdey guns and have been used by just about every other maker in one way or another. The other major style of engraving is to be seen most typically on Holland & Holland guns and consists of much bolder foliate scrolls on a hatched or matted ground. The boldness of this style lends itself to a 'brushed' finish whilst that used by Purdey's is normally 'colour hardened'. The most important development in engraving in recent decades (1950s to the present) has been in 'game' engraving. From the early naive game engraving that is so typical of nineteenth-century guns, game engraving has gradually evolved into a highly naturalistic means of decoration requiring great skill and artistry on the part of the engraver. More and more best guns are now engraved with game scenes and the present day excellence of those engravers associated with this development has led also to a general raising of the standards of classic engraving, from its nadir in the sixties. There are, of course, other refinements to be found on best guns, such as carved fences and gold-inlaid decoration, but more of this later.

The locks and action bodies of all guns will have their surfaces hardened after engraving. This process is essential as it protects the surface of the metal and the engraving. The colour-hardening process involves covering the surfaces of the steel with bone dust or leather, heating them, and then subjecting them to sudden cooling. If it is correctly done, it gives the metal a marvellous, fine finish of mottled blues, browns, greys, greens and other colours and it eases the visual transformation from the steel of the action to the wood of the stock. The colour wears off with use, so the amount retained by a gun, as long as it has not been re-coloured, is a good indication of how much use the gun has had and it is therefore a major determinant of value; one of the most commonly-asked questions in the gun trade concerns the percentage of 'colour' remaining on a gun.

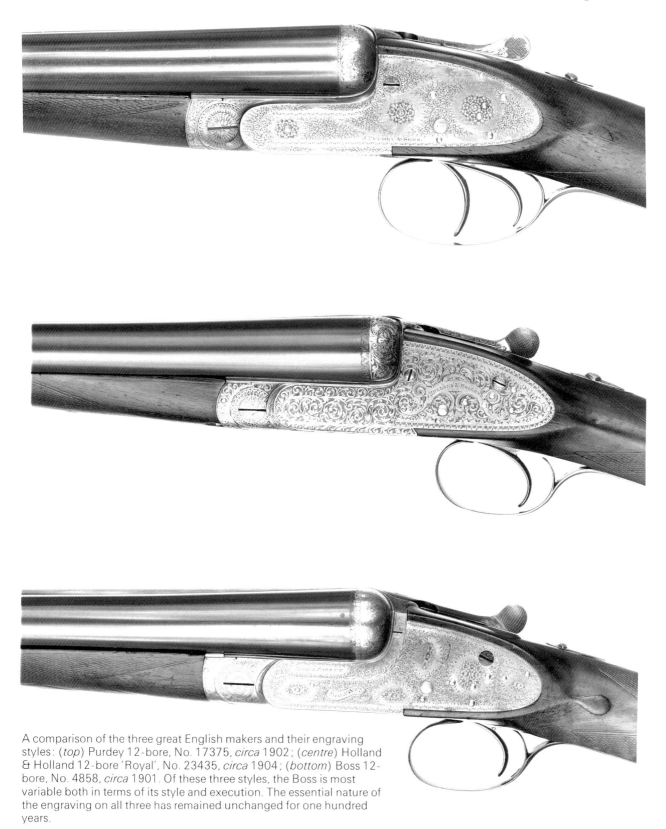

A comparison of the three great English makers and their engraving
styles: (*top*) Purdey 12-bore, No. 17375, *circa* 1902; (*centre*) Holland
& Holland 12-bore 'Royal', No. 23435, *circa* 1904; (*bottom*) Boss 12-
bore, No. 4858, *circa* 1901. Of these three styles, the Boss is most
variable both in terms of its style and execution. The essential nature of
the engraving on all three has remained unchanged for one hundred
years.

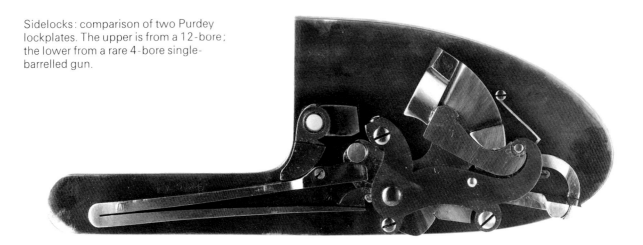

Sidelocks: comparison of two Purdey lockplates. The upper is from a 12-bore; the lower from a rare 4-bore single-barrelled gun.

New guns are given a layer of varnish to further protect the finish and it is a very good idea to re-varnish older guns that still retain their colour, for aesthetic as well as financial reasons.

Not all guns are given a colour-hardened finish – some are given a cyanide-hardened finish which does not add colour to the action; this method is, therefore, particularly suitable for guns with fine game engraving or very bold foliate-scroll engraving. The barrels and furniture are not hardened. As we have seen, Damascus barrels are browned, steel barrels are blued or blacked (some makers still refer to this latter procedure as browning). Both methods involve controlled rusting to eliminate the brightness of the metal and, ironically, to protect the surfaces from rusting. The finish achieved is dependent upon the careful preparation of the surfaces prior to treatment. Correct colour hardening and blueing are skilled procedures and their correct applications will impart great beauty to a best gun.

The features so far described are all now more or less standard on a best gun, but there will be other features, some routine, others added as a matter of personal taste. Self-opening mechanisms and single triggers can be classified as routine. Other features such as beavertail forends, unusual ribs, idiosyncratic stock configurations and gun weights will fall into the latter category. Self-

PLATE 1   A rare Kell-engraved 12 bore (2¾ in.) single-trigger self-opening sidelock ejector gun by J. Purdey, No. 23084. The gun was completed *circa* 1926 and, unusually, Purdey records note that the engraving was executed by Mr H. Kell, arguably the greatest of early twentieth-century engravers and the forefather of modern gun embellishment. The work was 'chased to match an existing gun, No. 20042' and resembles very closely the decoration on Purdey gun No. 14469, built in 1892 for the Shah of Persia. The gun was converted to single trigger by Purdey's in 1960.

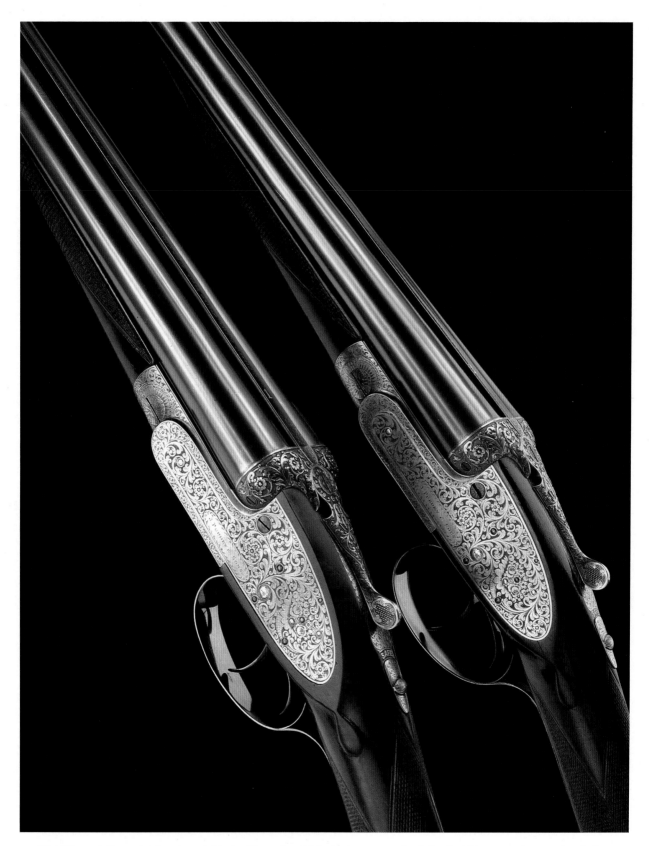

PLATE 2 A fine pair of 20-bore (2¾ in.) self-opening sidelock ejector guns by J. Purdey, No. 16617/8, completed *circa* 1900. Purdey records confirm the entry of these guns at the 1900 Paris Exposition and the work of embellishing the guns was almost certainly carried out by Barré, a French engraver working with Purdey's at this time. His work is clearly identifiable by the jewelled quality of the carving.

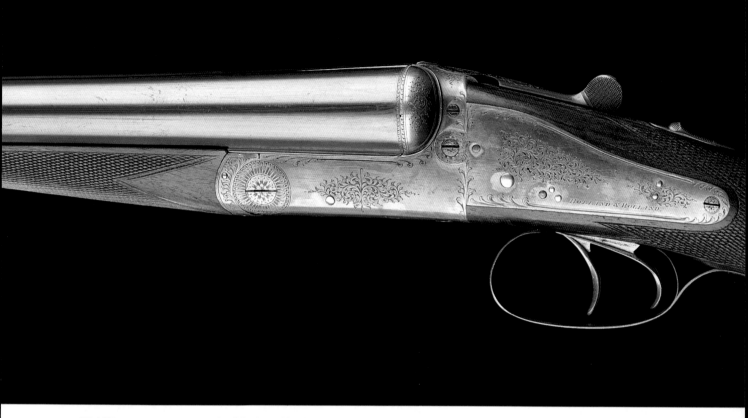

PLATE 3 A comparison of sidelock and back-action guns, (*above*) by Holland & Holland and (*below*) by Purdey's. Both are of exceptional quality and typical of the styles of their makers. Unlike Purdey's, Holland & Holland have made great use of back-action locks, especially in their double rifles where the demand for strength is imperative.

PLATE 4   A selection of best quality small-bore boxlock ejector guns. *From left to right:* a 28-bore boxlock ejector gun by W. Powell; a .410 boxlock ejector gun by Patstone; a .410 boxlock ejector gun by Watson. Boxlock ejector guns in the smaller bore sizes are not common and 28 and .410 examples are particularly sought after as boy's guns.

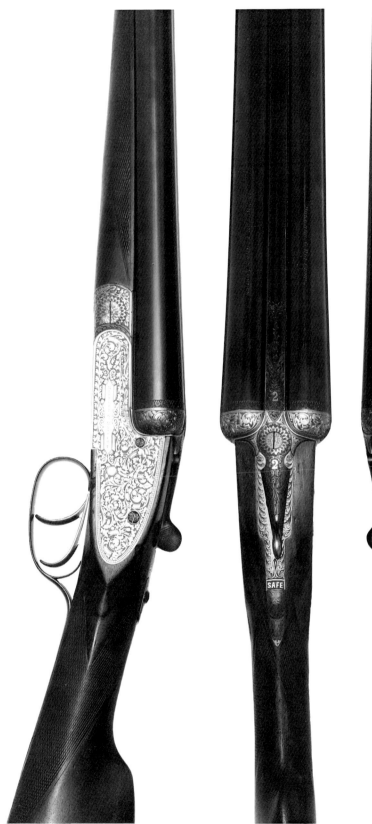

A set of three 12-bore
'Royal' sidelock ejector
guns by Holland &
Holland, No. 25055/6/7.

opening mechanisms, which are fairly common in side-by-sides but rare in over-and-under actions, are designed to enable a more rapid loading and firing of the gun and of all of them, the Purdey Beesley system is the most famous.

Purdey's are the only maker to have included a self-opening system on their best guns as a standard feature. The system used is very positive, kicking the barrels open with considerable force and requiring rather more effort in closing. It is one of the very few self-opening mechanisms which enables the gun to be opened with one hand, leaving the other free for loading and it is found also (with minor variations in design) on Atkin 'Spring Opener' guns and, very occasionally, on other maker's guns. I have recently, for example, seen a pair of Churchill 'Premiere' guns fitted with the same mechanism. Holland & Holland also make self-opener guns, but they have also, for many years, made other grades of best guns without self-openers. The full Boss self-opening system is something of a rarity and whilst virtually all Boss guns have an assisted-opening action as a result of the effect of the ejector-kickers on the forend pressing the extractors against the face of the action, the full self-opener is only normally fitted to their round-body guns (very roughly, 8000 series guns). All self-opener systems, with the exception of the Purdey, Rosson, Baker and Smith actions, tend to be more of a compromise in that whilst the self-opening action is not as fierce as say the Purdey action, they require less effort to close. The only disadvantage with some self-opening mechanisms is that they are not positive enough and in some new guns, where even a fierce system like the Purdey will take time to wear in because of the initial tightness of the jointing, the mechanism sometimes will not appear to be working positively enough.

It is common now to find single triggers fitted to best guns and the systems used can be divided fairly broadly into those built on the involuntary or three pull principle and those built on the inertia or delay principle. All three of the major gunmakers will supply single triggers; the Purdey design is normally non-selective, restricting firing to right and then right-left; the most commonly encountered Holland & Holland design is semi-selective enabling the left barrel to be fired after pushing the trigger forward. The Boss system is normally non-selective, but it can also be made fully-selective with the addition of a side-mounted selector slide. The mechanisms used by Boss & Woodward (and Purdey)

A Boss selective single trigger mechanism. The central pivot of the entire mechanism – the turret – can be seen situated in the centre of the trigger plate. Boss selective single triggers are scarce.

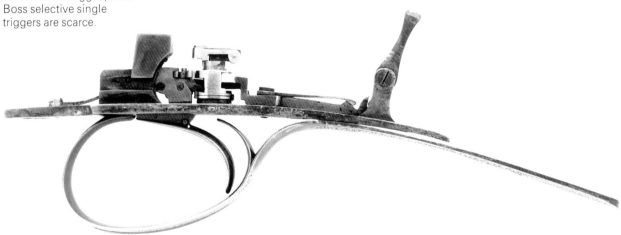

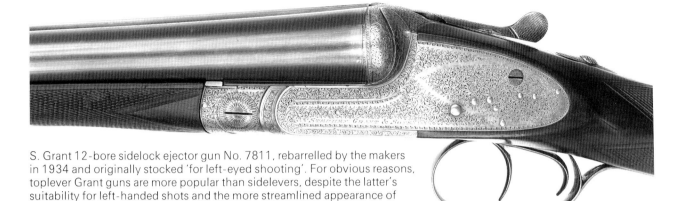

S. Grant 12-bore sidelock ejector gun No. 7811, rebarrelled by the makers in 1934 and originally stocked 'for left-eyed shooting'. For obvious reasons, toplever Grant guns are more popular than sidelevers, despite the latter's suitability for left-handed shots and the more streamlined appearance of sidelever guns. This gun bears the characteristic Grant decorative motifs of 'fluted' fences and close foliate-scroll engraving.

are based on the 'involuntary' pull system, the Boss trigger works on a rotating turret and the Woodward on a swinging arm. The Holland & Holland trigger uses a slide and operates on the 'delay' principle. In general, the overall market preference is for double triggers, but the last few decades have seen a growing appreciation of, and demand for, single triggers, particularly among those who take up game shooting after training in competitive clay shooting where single triggers are very much a standard feature. Preferences for the use of single triggers tend to be based upon the elimination of the need to move the forefinger from one trigger to the other which is often of great use to a beginner; the question of speed is largely academic. The use of a single trigger can help where gloves are worn or where bruising of the forefinger occurs with double triggers, but the fitting of a spring-bladed or articulated front trigger and a more spacious triggerguard on a double trigger gun would help just as well. Finally, one ingenious solution to the question as to whether to buy a single trigger or double trigger gun, is provided by Churchill's 'Special Repeating Trigger Mechanism'. In this action a stud behind the rear trigger controls the mechanism; a slight pressure on the stud from the left will convert the gun to a single trigger gun which can also be used as a double trigger gun whatever the position of the stud.

A Churchill 'Premiere' best grade gun. Relatively few guns are built with 'pinless' lockplates but the advantages of this idea as regards the decoration of a gun can quite clearly be seen in this illustration – there is an almost unbroken flow to the engraving. The 'full' engraving with no un-engraved areas is very much a Churchill feature on their Premiere grade guns.

Best engraving on a
Watson Bros sidelock
ejector gun. The engraving
is beautifully executed and
is typical of best guns by
this maker.

Best guns are built to individual specifications and whilst there is such a thing as a 'standard best', many guns will be encountered with added peculiarities. Top ribs can come in a variety of forms, occasionally sunk well down between the barrels, sometimes semi-sunken, or raised, and with a number of matted and filed finishes. A classic Churchill rib, for example, will have a high narrow profile with a matt surface. Some guns, particularly those by Boss and Churchill, will have a rolled edge triggerguard which allows the forefinger to lie more comfortably along the triggerguard; in some Churchill 'Premiere' grade guns, this rolled edge will be double, that is, added to both sides of the triggerguard, and it need not always be associated with a single trigger. An added refinement associated chiefly with Holland & Holland 'Royal' and 'Badminton' grade guns is the hand-detachable lock and the method used consists of a small lever, usually on the left lockplate, which is connected to a pin joining both lockplates; the removal of the lever and pin leaves the lockplates free to be gently tapped out. I have seen a similar refinement on only one pair of Purdey guns, but in this instance each lockplate had its own lever and pin.

Some best guns will be built with reinforced actions, with side bolsters, side clips and, unusually for guns of very high quality, top extensions. These are all features normally associated with guns built to withstand heavier loads. Classic Purdey 'pigeon' guns, for example, are built with side clips, which help to restrict any sideways 'play' in the barrels, and are given concealed third grips and heavier action bodies. Exceptions to the norm also include sidelevers, which are most often seen on Grant and occasionally Boss guns, lightweight actions such as those used on the Grant 'Lightweight', the Lancaster 'Twelve-Twenty' (a 12-bore gun with the weight advantage of a 20-bore), the Holland & Holland 'Brevis' and the Hellis 'Featherweight'.

2

Round Action and Over-and-Under Guns

I have dwelt at some length on the 'best' hammerless English sporting shotgun, treating it in its most commonly encountered form – as a double-barrelled, side-by-side sidelock, but there are two very distinct variations to this configuration. One is, by its very nature, a best gun. The other is a more general type and can be applied to best guns as easily as their more normal side-by-side configuration. We come, therefore, to the round action and the over-and-under sidelock gun. The round action or triggerplate action is a rather enigmatic design. For those new to guns, it can look rather like a boxlock and its action, whilst classified as 'best' is a clear link between the sidelock and boxlock. All the lockwork of a round action gun is situated on the triggerplate. There are, therefore, no lockplates, but occasionally a round action gun may be encountered which has dummy sideplates to disguise the triggerplate action. The term 'round action' should, incidentally, *not* be confused with 'round body' which is a shaping refinement found usually on Boss sidelocks; a 'rounded bar' can also be found on most sidelocks and usually consists of a curved shaping to the under edges of the action body. It is because the lockwork in a round action is no longer mounted on sideplates set into the sides of the action, but situated in the very centre of the gun on the triggerplate, that they are more slender and streamlined in appearance. The Scottish makers John Dickson and MacNaughton were the exclusive makers of round action guns, the design originating with MacNaughton. The guns are of marvellous workmanship and are usually of a very good weight – the nature of the design lending itself to the construction of lightweight guns. They have a devoted following but some sportsmen changing from sidelocks to round action guns have, I know, experienced problems adapting to the new type.

The elegant lines of a 12-bore round action ejector gun by J. Dickson. This gun was built at the turn of the century and illustrates how little the design of English guns has changed in the intervening ninety years.

(*This page and opposite*) Several views of a 'Superbritte' patent vertical-hinge side-opening over-and-under 12-bore 2¾ in. ejector gun by Jules Bury of Liège, No. 5094. The 'Superbritte' over-and-under action was patented in 1931 and was the invention of Théophile Britte of Vevegnis, near Liège. Some 250 'Superbritte' guns were produced and the basic principle is that of a side-by-side barrelled action turned on its right side so that the hinge pin is vertical and the barrels pivot open to the left, rather than downwards. Two English makers – Greener and Dickson's – claimed to have built early versions but such guns are rare.

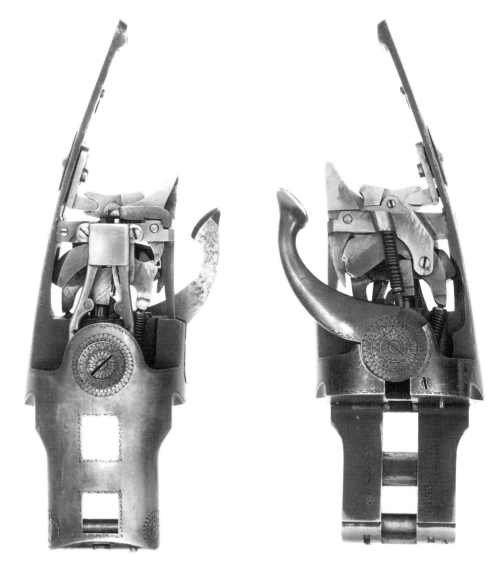

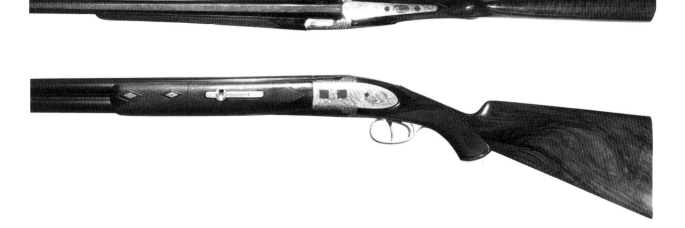

This, of course can happen at any time when guns are changed, but I believe that the problems in this instance incline to be associated with the centre of balance of a round action gun. In full sidelock guns there tends to be a greater concentration of weight in the centre of the gun, and this is particularly so with over-and-under guns. This concentration of weight in the centre can be a positive help in that it reduces the inertia of the barrels and stock and makes the gun more manoeuvrable. The centre of balance changes in a round action, and I believe it is possible for such guns to have increased inertia at either end. The lightness will make a great difference, of course, but the shift in balance can be startling. The round action will be encountered with or without ejectors, the later system of cocking/ejecting in Dickson guns adding a slight and incidental assisted-opening action. It is curious, but I have encountered more of these round action guns with Damascus barrels than any one type or make of sidelock. This may be a result of the obtaining of the original patent in 1880, when the use of Damascus was widespread.

Round action guns are becoming more and more sought after and now that Dickson's are producing this design again the older guns should become even more highly prized. Guns of this design have also, for some considerable time, been produced by David McKay Brown.

Over-and-under guns have for a long time been the subject of controversy, but the appearance of a gun of this type is now a very much accepted feature of the shooting field. Some people still have considerable objections to them because they feel that they are too clumsy in appearance and too heavy but the guns have a large and devoted following now, particularly in competitive shooting. The reasons for their popularity will be examined later on, but initially the designers of over-and-under guns had to overcome the problem of adapting this design to breech-loading guns. It is clear that a gun with greater vertical depth in the barrels will have design complexities, not only with its appearance, but

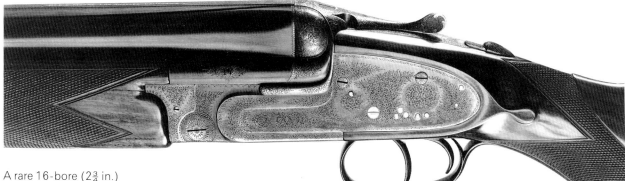

A rare 16-bore (2¾ in.) over-and-under sextuple-grip sidelock ejector pigeon gun by J. Purdey, No. 23055, built *circa* 1926. The illustration clearly shows the massive nature of such guns but they are an enduring tribute to the gun-making skills of their inventor, Harry Lawrence.

also with its 'gape' or the clearance of the breech ends and extractors from the action face. Many Continental over-and-under guns are unduly deep in the action because the barrel lumps are still situated directly under the bottom barrel, but the designers of English over-and-under guns (Boss and Woodward are justly famous in this respect) solved the problem by dividing the lumps and placing them on either side of the under barrel. There are other English patents where this is not the case and the guns therefore remain heavier and deeper in appearance. The action bars of over-and-under guns tend to be slightly longer than those of side-by-side guns because the extra length is required to help clear the barrels from the breech face. Over-and-under guns, do, I am quite certain, have advantages over side-by-side guns. They are probably quicker onto the target and possess greater 'pointability' because a narrower line is presented to the eye. Whilst their action bodies tend to be heavier, the concentration of weight in the centre of the gun will help its balance and it is well known that the U-section of the action imparts great strength. It has been shown also that the greater vertical rigidity of over-and-under barrels will reduce barrel 'flip' which occurs as the shot and pressures travel through the barrels and leave the muzzle.

The names of Boss and Woodward are those most normally associated with English over-and-under guns and the Woodward design is the basis of present-day Purdey over-and-under guns. The story of this particular design is an interesting one and involves a number of developments, from the over-and-under rifles of the late nineteenth century, through the early Purdey prototypes of the 1920s to the first fully developed Purdey over-and-under action which was built on a complex sextuple-grip principle. The sextuple-grip design comprised twin side lugs on the upper barrel and two pairs of side lumps on the lower barrel, providing six bites in all, and was developed by Harry Lawrence of Purdey's who had been inspired by the over-and-under gun made by Green's of Cheltenham. The so-called 'Green principle' possessed great strength and reliability, but involved much greater weight – guns built on this design would normally weigh between 8 lb and 8 lb 4 oz. The design also required unusually high standards of craftsmanship especially in the fitting of the barrels to the action. Because of the cost and time involved in building these sextuple-grip guns, relatively few were built by Purdey's and despite the introduction of a quadruple-grip modifica-

PLATE 5 A pair of 20-bore (2¾ in.) 'Model de Luxe Self-Opener' sidelock ejector guns by Holland & Holland, No. 40228/9. Engraved by Ken Hunt. The guns were built *circa* 1975 and comprised part of a set of eight, all consecutively numbered, of which six were engraved with bold acanthus scrollwork.

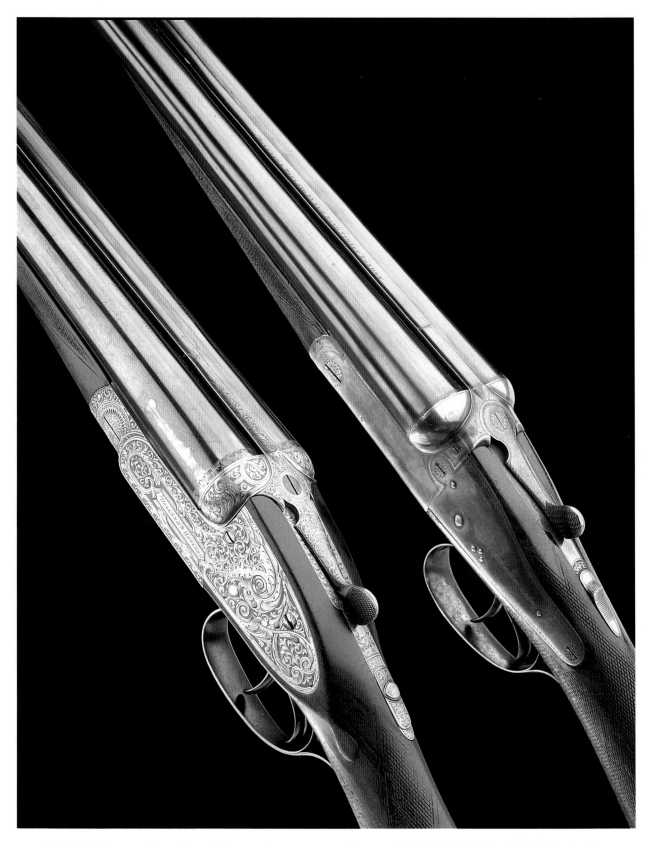

PLATE 6   A comparison of two distinct and contemporary 'house-styles'. *(left)* The Holland & Holland 12-bore (2¾ in.) 'Royal' sidelock ejector gun No. 22996 was completed *circa* 1902; *(right)* the 12-bore 'Dominion' backlock ejector gun No. 21003 was completed *circa* 1900 without engraving by the same maker.

tion, which effectively reduced the weight by $\frac{1}{2}$ lb, output was always very low. The quadruple-grip variation stands quite clearly between the earlier sextuple-grip action and the later Woodward/Purdey action in that the undue depth and heaviness of the earlier sextuple-grip actions were reduced by the simple expedient of eliminating the structural supports in the base of the earlier action. Strength was not compromised as the sides of the quadruple-grip action were thickened and the bolster at the external junction of the breech and bar was improved. A major reduction in the depth of the four barrel lumps led to a slender and more elegant action, but it was the elimination of the top-bites on the barrels that made the true quadruple-grip action. Such guns are rare, approximately ten being built during the thirties.

The real breakthrough in the design and production of Purdey over-and-under guns occurred when Purdey's acquired the Woodward gun-making concern in 1948. The Woodward design had long been renowned for its elegance and with the Boss action had, as mentioned, overcome the problem of an unduly deep action through the division and re-siting of the barrel lumps, producing an action body that was only marginally deeper than a side-by-side action body.

Purdey's abandoned their old designs, adopted the Woodward pattern and with certain modifications, produced the gun now known as the Purdey-Woodward over-and-under gun. The Purdey modifications included a small reduction in the width of the 12-bore ($2\frac{3}{4}$ in.) action and an important strengthening of the walls of the action, particularly at the radii – the junction between the breech face and the sides of the action body. Other modifications included a new design for the strikers, the introduction of stronger steel for the forend iron and the introduction of the Purdey bottom strap, safety slide and toplever.

There are, of course, other English over-and-under designs, and not all of

A Green patent lightweight over-and-under 12-bore backlock ejector gun by Edwinson Green, No. 6854. The inspiration for Purdey's sextuple-grip over-and-under, the Green principle is a quadruple-grip action with a double underbolt, twin side bites and a canted crossbolt.

A 12-bore (2¾ in.) 'Ovundo' over-and-under boxlock ejector gun by Westley Richards, No. 17924, built *circa* 1940 with hand-detachable locks, a fully selective single trigger and with hinged inspection ports in the dummy sideplates.

them are sidelocks. The Westley Richards 'Ovundo', for example, is an over-and-under gun built on Anson and Deeley boxlocks which are also hand-detachable, in a design exclusive to Westley Richards. The 'Ovundo' is also a disguised box-lock as it is fitted with dummy sideplates – these usually have inspection ports which, on opening, reveal the internal action.

Over-and-under guns have also been produced by Beesley, Edwinson Green, Holland & Holland, Lancaster, Lang, Churchill and others. The Churchill over-and-under action resembles the Woodward in having the hooks and bites of the barrels at the sides, which permits an elegantly shallow action body. With the exception of late production Purdey and Holland & Holland guns, however, those built by Boss and Woodward alone combine the most desirable character-istics of this particular configuration – elegance of design, reliability of the action, particularly in relation to the clearance of the strikers from the action face, effi-ciency and ease in the manner of assembly and disassembly (particularly with the Boss) and the greater provision of 'gape' to facilitate ease of loading. It is also of interest to note that many over-and-under guns are fitted with hold-open top-levers which help greatly with the assembly of the gun. With this device the toplever remains in its open position as the barrels are fitted in and it shuts as the barrels operate on a small stud at the base or face of the standing breech on closing.

The late Sir Joseph Nickerson, who was an early exponent of the use of over-and-under guns, always maintained that over-and-under guns made him quicker onto the target and a lifetime of remarkably accurate shooting bears testimony

A 20-bore over-and-under sidelock ejector gun by Boss, No. 7013, with a fully-selective single trigger. The Boss selector is shown to the rear of the left lock plate. Note also the impressed Whitworth trade mark on the over barrel.

to this. The sale of his collection of sporting guns at Christie's on 13 March 1991 included a number of his over-and-under guns. One of them, a Purdey 12-bore No. 26113A, was completed *circa* 1949 and together with a pair of Purdey 16-bore guns Nos 26111/2 was among the first of the Purdey over-and-under guns built on the Woodward design. Sir Joseph also used Woodward guns and the sale included four of these guns, covering the years 1922, 1923, 1925 and 1947.

There seems now to be a general acceptance of over-and-under guns particularly as more people have come to understand the extraordinary quality of the best English variations. More and more of these guns have become vehicles for the gun-engravers art, especially in recent times, but there can be no doubt that for many enthusiasts, the pinnacle of achievement for this particular configuration occurred in the twenties and thirties, and found its essence in the Boss and Woodward designs.

A 12-bore 'Ovundo' by Westley Richards, No. 18072. Work on the gun was commenced *circa* 1927 but it appears not to have been completed until 1935. The gun has been stripped of its dummy sideplate with its hinged inspection port; the lock work of the detachable boxlocks is clearly shown and the patent W.R. 'One-Trigger' single trigger mechanism is set to fire the right lock.

3

Boxlocks and Other Sidelocks

Our discussion so far has concerned itself with best quality sidelocks, but a collector of fine English guns would do well to consider so-called second and third quality sidelocks, and of course, boxlocks. Many makers produced lower grade sidelocks for those who could not afford a best gun, or for those who simply wanted a more workaday firearm. Many, for obvious reasons, were supplied to the colonies, hence the origin of Lancaster's 'Colonial' grade guns, and the Army & Navy production. Churchill, for example, produced 'Imperial' and 'Field' grade sidelocks which are identified, in the occasional absence of a grade marking, by somewhat less engraving, a more general use of dovetail as opposed to chopper lumps, and by a generally more routine finish. A large proportion of early sidelocks are of this type and they are usually identified by the use of Webley actions with their 'horseshoe' toplever and spindle and their 'through' lump projecting through to the underside of the action body. But there are many other second quality sidelocks which were built with chopper lumps and finished to a very high standard indeed. In addition to the makers and grades already mentioned, Holland & Holland produced 'Badminton' and 'No. 2 Grade' guns which are essentially best guns with somewhat less finish and we should not forget their 'Dominion' backlock guns, that were, and still are, renowned for their quality and exceptional strength.

Purdey's also sold five different qualities of gun, from their best to 'D' and 'E' Quality. The latter were guns bought from the trade and then stocked, finished and shot and regulated by Purdey's in much the same way that Holland & Holland sold 'Shot and Regulated' guns. Guns bought by Purdey's from other makers, in their entirety and for sale to Purdey customers, were given an 'A' prefix number and cover every type, from Winchester and Colt longarms to

A 12-bore boxlock ejector gun by W. Evans, No. 7319, with two additional de luxe finishes. The pin at the upper edge of the action body indicates that the gun has been fitted with an intercepting safety – a less commonly encountered feature for a boxlock and considerable care has been taken in the carving of the fences. Note also the shaping of the forend wood just beyond the 'knuckle' of the action.

A rare lightweight 12-bore single trigger boxlock ejector gun by W. Ford, No. 5300. The gun is fitted with a Boss selective single trigger with its side-mounted selector. The gun was formerly owned by C.W.P. Hampton (1913–1991), an outstanding collector of vintage motor cars who lost the use of his left arm as the result of being badly wounded in the Second World War. This disability is almost certainly the reason for this gun's conversion to single trigger and the choice of a lightweight gun is also particularly fitting.

revolvers and automatic pistols. All other English makers produced sidelocks of varying types. In general, second and third quality guns can be identified in a number of ways. Most will have a top extension of one sort or another, varying from simple straight and concealed extensions, to more complex doll's head and bolted extensions with cross-bolts of round and square section. They will also, normally, be built with dovetail, drop, through and table lumps, not chopper lumps, and very many were built on Webley actions which, as we have seen, have a distinctive horseshoe spindle and toplever, and a through lump. Many will not be stocked to the fences, but this is sometimes a feature of early 'best' quality guns and in many cases is simply a more archaic design.

The engraving on guns of this type will vary from excellent (especially if they come from 'small' little known makers who wanted to produce something different from their normal range of boxlocks), to good, to barely adequate. The quality and quantity would also differ according to when the guns were built. Cogswell & Harrison, for example, produced very many sidelock guns, with those built during the twenties, thirties and forties/fifties generally having a rather good finish, but with those produced in the machine-dominated sixties usually having a very poor finish indeed. However, finish, whilst being of critical importance to an expensive best gun, should not detract from the general worthiness and value for money of these guns. I have devoted a later chapter to questions of relative value and it is therefore sufficient here simply to remark that there are very many good, attractive and reliable second and third quality sidelocks to be found and many of them will find a good home in a small but representative collection illustrating the production of British gunmakers over the last century or so.

The question of value leads us directly on to a discussion of boxlocks, for the sum of money required to buy a moderate quality sidelock in average to poor condition, and therefore requiring a possible future outlay for repairs and corrections, will still buy an excellent boxlock ejector gun in very good condition. The classic English boxlock differs considerably, in both nature and appearance, from the sidelock. This type of action is now almost invariably built on the

An 8-bore (3¼ in.) boxlock ejector gun by Ogden, Smiths & Hussey, No. 10006. This gun is of very high quality but, in keeping with many guns built for wild-fowling, was given a minimum of ornamentation. It retains much of its original colour hardening.

Anson & Deeley design (1875) in which the locks are inserted *into* the body of the action; they are not, therefore, carried on separate lockplates as they are with sidelocks, but occasionally, boxlocks will be found with dummy sideplates which are fitted and engraved to disguise the action and Cogswell & Harrison guns are of particular note in this respect. The normal appearance, however, is rather like a box, hence the name, with the rear of the action body ending in a distinct straight line from the fences to the triggerplate. In higher grade boxlocks, the rear of the action body is frequently given a more ornate shape; Churchill and Westley Richards boxlocks, for example, are sometimes given a scroll back, while other makers such as Atkin, Evans, Jeffries and Wilkes will often use scallop-backed and ogee-backed action bodies.

In keeping with sidelock guns, ejectors are very much a standard feature, but more non-ejector boxlocks will be encountered because the boxlock was a very much cheaper type. Occasionally, these non-ejector variants will be of very high quality indeed, but it is far more normal for them to be plain or of average quality. The ejector systems usually encountered are normally of the Deeley or Southgate types, but of course, there will be variations on this. The same will be true of the opening and bolting systems which are normally the Scott spindle and Purdey bolt, and Westley Richards guns will be found with their patent lift-up toplever and their earliest boxlock guns will be fitted with a single lump to the barrels but this is now an obsolete feature.

It would be a mistake to suppose that makers did not put a great deal of effort into their boxlocks. Smaller and less well-known makers would sometimes produce a number of extremely highly-finished boxlocks to demonstrate their gunmaking skills. Best quality boxlocks are characterized by an unusually high degree of finish, with best foliate-scroll engraving, scroll-back action bodies, self-opening and single trigger systems and chopper lump barrels. They will not normally have top extensions unless they are by Greener, and they will have any number of refinements such as decorative chequering, highly-figured wood and lightweight action bodies.

Any discussion of boxlock guns must involve Greener and Westley Richards, for both made an enormous contribution to their development. Greener remains famous for his 'Facile Princeps' boxlock action in which the cocking of the tumblers is achieved by an extension to the forward lump of the barrels and, of course, for his 'Unique' action in which the mainsprings are used to operate both the ejectors and the tumblers. W.W. Greener was a great advocate of the top extension and he devoted considerable time and resource to demonstrating how accurate workmanship was vital in their effective use. The normal Greener 'safe' is also distinctive and it resembles more closely the safety devices often found on Continental combination guns where it appears as a side safe, whether manual or automatic, let into the side of the head of the stock.

The contribution made by Westley Richards is very great indeed. Above all else, they are famous for inventing hand-detachable locks for boxlocks. These are carried on separate plates and are inserted into the action body from the underside. The bottom plate of the action body which, in other boxlocks, is screwed or pinned in place is, on these 'drop-lock' guns, fitted with a chequered press catch on its forward edge so that it can be removed completely or hinged down to allow the removal of the locks. This design makes it easier to remove the locks for repair and maintenance but there is, nevertheless, a strong case for making the working parts of a gun unavailable to curious and prying fingers. The same can be said of hand-detachable sidelocks. Westley Richards hand-detachable locks are invariably beautifully built and finished and guns with this feature are now very highly sought after indeed. The same is true of Greener 'Royal' grade boxlocks which are finished with the addition of some goldwork in the engraving, and with barrels of best grade steel with scroll-engraved breech ends. Greener guns are normally marked with a grade which is to be found at the very end of the triggerguard tang or bottom strap; the designation 'FH 35', for example, will indicate a Facile Princeps gun costing 35 guineas.

A 12-bore 'Grade G60 Royal' Facile Princeps boxlock ejector gun by W.W. Greener, No. 53146; the gun is richly embellished with arcaded fences, a scroll back action body, and de luxe engraving. Note the typical Greener side safe.

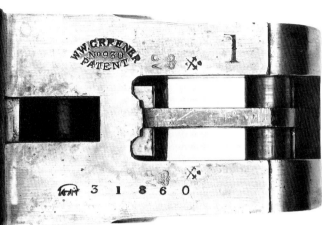

The 'water table' or action bar of a 'Royal' grade boxlock non-ejector gun by W.W. Greener. The gun is the No. 1 of a pair, No. 31860/1, built *circa* 1886/7 and it features an unusual variant of Greener's 'Facile Princeps' action, with two front barrel lumps in parallel, each incorporating a cocking rod and having a separate slot in the bar table. The rear barrel lump is standard, and the breech locking system comprises a Purdey bolt engaging each lump and a Greener 'Wedge Fast' top bolt. Note also the Greener elephant trademark.

A 12-bore 'Grade F.H. Special' boxlock ejector gun by W.W. Greener, No. 65164, completed *circa* 1918–1920. The gun is a fine example of Greener's best quality.

A 12-bore (2¾ in.) 'Royal' grade 'Unique' boxlock ejector gun by W.W. Greener, No. 49643. Built on a scroll back action body, the gun has fences carved with a shell motif and an ornately decorated stock with horn inserts and 'fancy' border chequering.

Churchill boxlock guns are also given grade names chief among which are the 'Regal', 'Hercules', 'Utility', 'Crown' and 'Prodigy' grades. The Regal and Hercules guns are of the very best quality, the Utility being sold as the Regal after the Second World War. The name was changed in the post-war years as it was by then associated with cheap or poor quality goods. Virtually all British makers produced boxlock guns, many of them using Webley '700' actions which are to be identified by their 'horseshoe' toplevers and through lumps. Webley and Scott have always been famous for their production of boxlocks with the '700' being their standard model but they also produced much more highly-finished guns such as the '701' and '702' models. In keeping with other makers, Holland & Holland would buy actions in from the trade and sell the finished guns as 'Shot and Regulated' guns and Holland's modern production of boxlocks has included the 'Cavalier' and 'Northwood' grades. Boss are alone in not having produced boxlock guns but as in just about every other thing associated with the English gun trade, anomalies do exist. Whilst Boss might maintain that they have only ever made sidelocks, occasionally boxlocks will be encountered with the Robertson name – John Robertson was the factory manager at Boss for many years. Purdey and Woodward built some boxlocks, but these are relatively rare.

The rugged and utilitarian nature of most boxlocks, however, means that they were ideal for use under rough or adverse conditions, where to use an expensive best gun would be unwise. They are therefore often encountered as wildfowling guns, in all bore sizes from 12 ($2\frac{3}{4}$ in.) and 12 (3in. Magnum) up to 10 and 8 where they are normally not fitted with ejectors. At the same time, the very nature of the boxlock action, where more of the interior of the action body is machined out to take the lockwork means that they are ideal as lightweight guns.

Recent years have seen something of a resurgence in the popularity of lightweight guns built for 2 in. and $2\frac{1}{2}$ in. cartridges and many of these were completed with a very high degree of finish. One example recently encountered had Whitworth steel chopper lump barrels, an exceptionally pretty action and stock and a Boss single trigger with a rolled edge triggerguard. Boss advertised the conversion of double trigger guns to their patent single trigger on their trade labels and whilst this seems to have been carried out, in the main, on sidelocks, some boxlocks were obviously deemed worthy of the expense as well.

Another example of the very rugged nature of boxlock guns is the 'Duplex' boxlock, a Webley & Scott Grade 3 proprietary pigeon gun, introduced by Holland & Holland during the First World War. It had a two stage choke boring, and with its special chain-shot cartridges, it was adopted for use by the Admiralty in 1915 as a means of attacking the fabric and frames of enemy aircraft.

The history of Greener's St George gun is a fitting end to this chapter, for it illustrates the great efforts that were often devoted to boxlocks; the following extract is by Christopher Brunker and is taken from a Christie's sale catalogue:

'According to Leyton Greener's history, the legend of the "St George" began *circa* 1880 when a pair of best Damascus barrels were accidentally shortened

One of a pair of 12-bore boxlock ejector guns by W. Powell, No. 10406/7. In keeping with much gunmaking practice at the time, these guns were subsequently fitted with Boss single triggers. The more unusual location of the safety device is a later alteration.

and rejected. About ten years later, it was decided to build a "show gun" and the rejected tubes were used for it. It is not known who originated the idea, but it was quite probably W.W. Greener himself.

'However, the project became the personal responsibility of his son, Harry Greener, who designed the embellishment. The "inertia weight" single trigger used on the gun was also one of Harry's designs (1882). The stock he fashioned himself, deliberately choosing an exotic blank of Circassian walnut that had been rejected for having too many natural faults. Each fault had to be removed and plugged with a precisely-shaped insert of wood. Leyton estimated that there were over 100 inserts, none of which came loose despite heavy use. The stock was unchequered, this being a Greener preference and a "trigger locking device" was omitted to emphasise that only unloaded guns are safe.

'Harry Tomlinson "a first class engraver and in-layer" was given the task of "carving the forged steel". He was told to work on the gun only "when he felt inclined", but on two occasions the strain led to his becoming "overtaxed . . . until he was served with alcohol in the P.H. opposite the factory gates; there he remained for several days".

'The gun appears to have been completed in 1903, which accords with its serial number 52227. Harry Greener had great success with "the show gun" in the sporting field and the value of this was acknowledged by W.W. Greener on his retirement in 1910 when he presented the gun to Harry, in whose hands, he said, it had been "the best advertisement so far tried". After the gun became his property, Harry renamed it "The St George" in preference to "The Show Gun".

'A second gun with identical decoration appears to have been built in the early 1900s. It is illustrated in Greener's *The Gun and Its Development* (1910), facing p. 278, and is captioned "The Highest Development of the Sporting Gun . . . 1907". The gun shown has double triggers, a side safe and chequered stock, and is said to have been lost at sea in transit to the buyer, a Persian noble. According to Greener's records, the design was not repeated and "The St George is now unique".'

(See page 116 for illustrations of the St George gun.)

4

Hammer Guns

and those guns illustrating the development of the Modern English Gun

Hammer guns and those guns with unusual actions provide a most varied and interesting area for the collector of English sporting guns and there seems now to be a growing interest in the origins of the sporting gun amongst those buyers who have, for a long time, devoted themselves to the acquisition of the fully-formed and perfected 'late' types; best guns will be encountered here, as will many others of exceptional character and quality.

The period 1850 to 1900 saw the beginnings and final perfection of the modern English sporting gun, from its earlier origins in the flintlock and percussion guns of the eighteenth and nineteenth centuries. This was an age of great fertility of ideas and of the imaginative and daring exploration of methods of construction across the entire industrial network of the country. For the inventor of new ideas with regard to sporting guns, the entire thrust was to create a more practical, safer and speedier method of loading and firing a gun but there was rarely ever an entirely clean break with the past; in the decades that led, inexorably, to the development of the hammerless sporting gun of today, there was a reluctance to put aside the more familiar characteristics of the guns that had gone before. Thus we find that the design and function of the lockwork for the firing mechanisms remained essentially unchanged and that the manufacture of the barrels and stocks of guns continued largely as it had done in the years preceding these

An example of the rather more interesting aspects of early hammer guns, this Jeffries 1862 Second patent side-opening 12-bore hammer gun is one of a number of early experiments with breech-loading guns. Needless to say, such guns are now scarce and generate considerable interest among collectors.

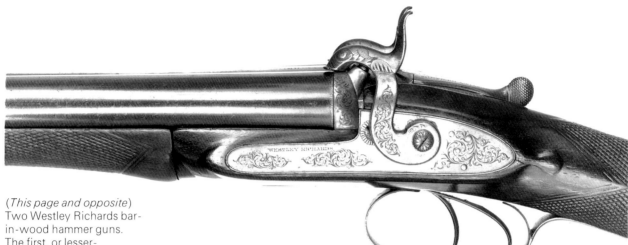

(*This page and opposite*) Two Westley Richards bar-in-wood hammer guns. The first, or lesser-engraved gun is built on Westley Richards 1864 patent, the second on the 1871 patent. Each has the bar-in-wood extending to cover the forend hinge in a 'crab joint'.

developments. We find also the retention of other practical and decorative features such as percussion fences, and whilst the size of the foliate-scroll engraving on the lockplates and furniture became somewhat reduced, the forms of the decoration also remained largely unchanged.

These factors, however, are largely incidental to the major development of the mid nineteenth century: the introduction of an entirely new way of loading a gun. Previously, the method had been to introduce the charge of powder, wad and shot via the muzzle of the gun, the charge then being ignited by means of the flintlock, and later by the percussion cap. Whilst the percussion cap was a major improvement on the flintlock, it had, by comparison with the new cartridge-firing breech-loading designs some major disadvantages. It was, for example, slow and cumbersome to use, the firer being frustrated in his pursuit of 'rough' game by the need to stop, place the butt of the gun on the ground and load from the muzzle. The muzzle-loading systems were also quite dangerous – it was always possible to load on top of a previous charge, and there was no guarantee that there would not be a piece of glowing tow left in the barrel when the charge was introduced.

The introduction of the pin-fire gun, which, for our purposes, was the earliest major form of the breech-loading gun, effectively dismissed the majority of the disadvantages associated with percussion guns. The new idea spread to England from France where Lefaucheux had produced a breech-loading gun which was designed to use a cartridge developed by Houllier in 1850 and the basic idea was very simple: a pin projecting from the base of the cartridge was attached to an internal percussion cap and the descending hammer would drive the pin downwards into the cap to effect the detonation of the charge.

This new breech-loading system was the first major introduction of the idea of carrying individual self-contained cartridges which were designed to be inserted into the breech ends of the barrels; it meant that loads could be changed swiftly according to the circumstances of the shoot. It also heralded a quicker and cleaner use of the gun, for the barrels could be opened and closed in a fraction

of the time it took to load a muzzle-loading gun and, moreover, they could be viewed properly for marks and deposit.

The pin-fire system had one disadvantage – the projecting pin could be given an accidental blow which would, of course, ignite the charge and pin-fire guns tend, in general, to be rather cumbersome and are seldom as elegant as the later centre-fire guns. Nevertheless, the short life of the pin-fire makes the system of interest to the collector as pin-fire guns represent an important but now obscure development in the history of the sporting gun.

The identification of a pin-fire gun is quite simple; it will, of course, have external hammers and the breech ends of the barrels will have slots to take the pins of the cartridges, which will project above the surface of the barrel as they are loaded.

With differences of design excepted, pin-fire guns will, generally, still incorporate certain of the characteristics to be found on muzzle-loading percussion guns. The barrels will be of Damascus or any one of a variety of 'twists' depending upon the quality of the gun. The very best Damascus barrels have highly distinctive and very intricate patterns which required considerable gunmaking skills to manufacture; the Holland & Holland collection, for example, contains a number of fine examples of Damascus tubes, one of which incorporates the name of the barrel-maker in the patterning. 'Twist' barrels are generally much less ornate in appearance, the patterning often consisting of widely spaced striations and they are usually to be found on guns of average or poor quality. The shape of the hammers of pin-fire guns will also retain the general shape of those to be found on percussion guns, many taking the shape of stylized dolphins with high or low spurs according to the tastes and style of the gunmaker and some can have a very high 'rabbit-eared' appearance.

Another problem sometimes encountered with pin-fire guns concerned the removal of the cartridge after firing which could become jammed in the breech. Some later guns will, therefore, be found with recesses on the undersides of the

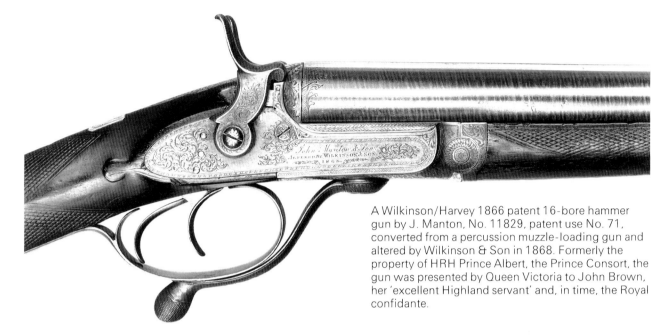

A Wilkinson/Harvey 1866 patent 16-bore hammer gun by J. Manton, No. 11829, patent use No. 71, converted from a percussion muzzle-loading gun and altered by Wilkinson & Son in 1868. Formerly the property of HRH Prince Albert, the Prince Consort, the gun was presented by Queen Victoria to John Brown, her 'excellent Highland servant' and, in time, the Royal confidante.

hammers which would hook over the projecting pin to enable the spent case to be drawn clear of the chambers.

There were many attempts to improve upon the original Lefaucheux system and pin-fire guns will therefore be found with a number of interesting technical changes. Joseph Lang was the first English gunmaker to appreciate the advantage of the 'new' system over the old muzzle-loading guns and he was quick to introduce his own version of it. The Lefaucheux idea provided for the barrels of the gun to be hinged open on the operation of the underlever; a system introduced by Bastin involved sliding the barrels forward on the operation of the underlever and there were other systems using rotary underlevers or providing for the forward and downward movement of the barrels on opening.

In addition to experiments with methods of opening and the extraction of the fired cartridge, there were also attempts to improve the strength of pin-fire actions and to bring about a more efficient method of closure. Self-cocking and self half-cocking patents were introduced which helped to solve the problem of having to bring the hammers to half cock before the barrels could be opened.

The collector will also encounter pin-fire guns that are conversions from the percussion era and there are scarcer types such as 'hammerless' guns disguised as pin-fire hammer guns in which the sidelocks have manual cocking levers that take the form of pin-fire hammers; drawing the external pin-fire hammers to half or full cock has a corresponding action on the internal hammers.

Pin-fire guns were made by all the English gunmakers of the day and by many other smaller and less well-known makers; the system was widely spread throughout Europe and there are many best quality examples to be found.

The period of the pin-fire gun was, by gunmaking standards, brief, lasting from about 1850 to the mid-1860s. The introduction of the centre-fire cartridge by George Daw in 1861 set the evolution of the sporting gun firmly on its true course and brought about the demise of more cumbersome systems. The centre-fire cartridge was yet another idea that had originated in France, the initial Pottet invention receiving modifications by Schneider. Daw introduced this later version to England, at the same time claiming exclusive rights to the idea, a claim that was successfully challenged by Eley. The resulting freedom from the controls imposed by a patent meant that the idea became public property and other gunmakers were quick to grasp the opportunity to produce their own modifications of the centre-fire principle.

There are a number of excellent guides to the huge quantity of patents that were brought out at this time and a number of interesting collections have been established around the objective of selecting a good example of each of the major designs; our purpose here is to examine those characteristics which became pre-eminent and by which good hammer guns can be recognized.

The centre-fire hammer gun flourished over a period of not more than about three decades, very roughly from the 1860s to the mid 1880s and it formed the link between the very earliest breech-loading guns, including base-fire and needle-fire guns, and the modern hammerless guns. Some hammer guns continued to be made into this century, particularly those made as boy's or keeper's guns but there were some people, particularly the great shots of the Edwardian era, who continued to use hammer guns well into the twentieth century; Lord de Grey, later 2nd Marquess of Ripon, to whom half a million head of game fell in his lifetime, continued to use his trios of Purdey hammer and hammer ejector guns into the 1920s. There were still others, such as the eccentric collector Charles Gordon, who were obviously unable to accept fully the innovation of the hammerless guns, and who continued to order hammer guns from the leading makers of the day. Charles Gordon did not use the guns he amassed and he is chiefly associated with John Dickson & Son of Edinburgh, who built numerous shotguns, rifles and pistols for him, all of fine quality and distinctively cased. Gordon will be remembered most for his fondness for ordering flintlock and percussion guns from this maker and Dickson's seem to have surpassed themselves in catering to his rather peculiar tastes – at a time when their hammerless

A late, fully-developed 12-bore hammer gun by W.R. Pape, No. 3503 incorporating Pape's 1874 patent, with rebounding sidelocks and a toplever. Late hammer guns such as this are the most desirable of their type.

gun production was in full swing. Charles Gordon is believed to have ordered his first gun from Dickson's in 1875 and, though this was a breech-loading centre-fire (12-bore, No. 2770), a high proportion of his subsequent orders were for muzzle-loaders; he died in 1904, owing Dickson's, it is believed, a fortune.

But what are the characteristics to look for in the most collectable hammer guns? With other interesting factors such as provenance excepted, the most desirable features are similar to those associated with best hammerless guns. They should, for example, be streamlined in appearance, with each component part in overall harmony; and they should be practical, which explains the market's current fondness for late production hammer guns incorporating the most developed features of the period. We will find therefore that toplever hammer guns incorporating the Scott spindle of 1865 and the Purdey bolt of 1870 are very popular, particularly amongst those buyers who will, the condition of the gun permitting, be using the gun.

The mention of condition is very important and it is quite rare now to find hammer guns in anything approaching excellent condition. Those that retain a good proportion of their original colour hardening and blueing will be of particular interest to collectors; when one remembers that most of these guns have seen significant use for a period of more than a hundred years and that they became quickly neglected when new designs were introduced, it is something of a pleasure to find any hammer gun in good, crisp condition.

The most collectable best hammer guns will have bar-action sidelocks which, as we have seen previously, are generally more expensive to fit. A great number of best hammer guns, however, are fitted with back-action lockplates which may or may not be connected to the action body; this is as much the case with Purdey guns as it is with any of the other makers. Another added refinement is the 'bar-in-wood' in which the entire underside of the action body, extending to the 'knuckle' of the action, is encased in the stock wood. In certain guns by Westley Richards, the wood of the forend will also entirely overlap the forend-iron in what is called a 'crab' joint, giving the underside of the gun, with the exception of the furniture, the appearance of being constructed entirely of walnut. Both are very much de luxe features, as the fitting of the wood to the metal requires, as indeed does 'best' stock work in general, the skills of a cabinet-maker.

The earliest hammer guns had non-rebounding locks, thereby necessitating the withdrawal of the hammers to half cock before the gun could be opened,

One of a pair of 12-bore bar-in-wood hammer guns by J. Purdey, No. 10008/9, built *circa* 1877. The guns incorporate Purdey's 1863 patent snap action underlever with the addition of this most unusual French-style scroll.

PLATE 7 *(above)* The pair of 'Conan the Barbarian' guns by J. Roberts in their oak and leather case, with engraving by Ken Hunt. *(below)* A 12-bore (2¾ in.) over-and-under sidelock ejector gun by Boss with fully selective single-trigger and, for Boss, a most unusual engraving style which is closer in character to Holland & Holland guns.

PLATE 8   A set of three 12-bore sidelock ejector guns by Boss in their tiered and brass mounted oak and leather triple case.

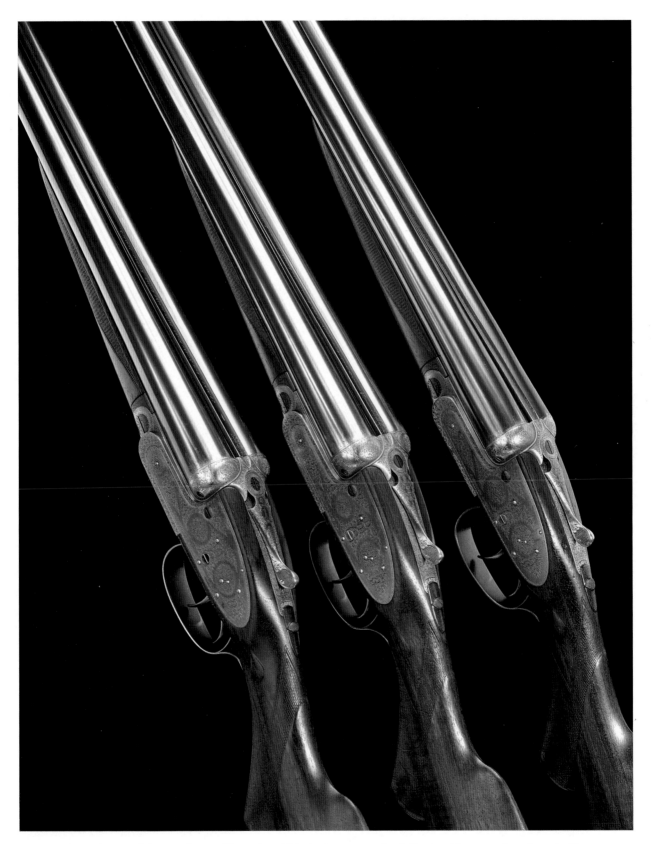

PLATE 9 A set of three 12-bore self-opening sidelock ejector guns by J. Purdey, No. 24941/2 and 25063. True sets of three guns are not common and it is more usual to encounter sets in which one gun has been built at a later date to match the pair. Guns No. 24941/2 were completed in 1935 and gun No. 25063 was built in the same year as the third gun to the set.

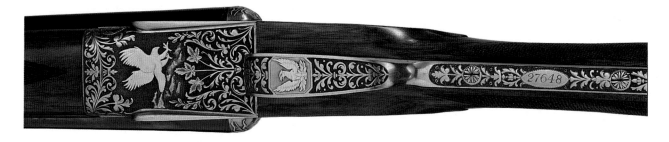

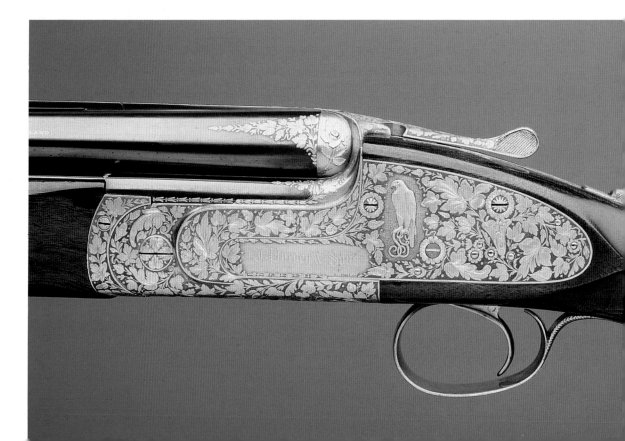

PLATE 10
Engraved and
gold-encrusted
masterpieces by
the renowned
Ken Hunt.

but subsequent developments introduced the rebounding lock in which the hammer returns slightly upon hitting the striker and this meant a less clumsy action and a faster loading of the gun. Today it is a good indication of the stage of development of each gun, as are the methods of fastening the forend and the strengthening of the action.

In the first instance, the use of the Anson push-rod or the Deeley catch will indicate late production, but the most commonly used method before the mid-1870s and the advent of these two patents was a simple bolt fastening, situated about two-thirds of the way up the forend and consisting of a bolt that was pushed through the forend and forend loop on the barrels. The respective merits of these various methods will be quickly appreciated in use, and whilst it is not normal to have to take the forend off when the gun is in actual use, the simple bolt-fastening usually requires somewhat more than a thumb-nail to operate, particularly if the fit is tight; the other two are fast and easy.

One very important addition to the strength of hammer gun actions was the introduction of a 'radius' at the junction of the breech face and the action bar. In the earliest guns, this is usually a more or less right-angled junction which will not impart great strength to that part of the action body which needs it most; this is the part of the action body that is most susceptible to serious cracks because it is at this point that the flexing and bending pressures that are created when the gun is fired will exert themselves most fully. The addition of a radius will therefore indicate a gun of later manufacture. Hammerless guns, unless they are of the earlier and more unusual types, will always have a radius at this point.

We can, therefore, summarize the desirable features as follows: for a gun that is to be used as well as appreciated for its aesthetic qualities, it should be of later production, preferably with a toplever and whilst Damascus barrels are very much the norm for all hammer guns, original steel barrels are rather desirable because people feel more confident with them. The arguments over Damascus versus steel are quite simple; Damascus is essentially a combination of two metals and the method of construction sometimes permitted the creation

A fine 12-bore hammer gun by J. Purdey, No. 9304. This gun embodies all the late fully-developed characteristics of a hammer gun. It has a toplever, rebounding sidelocks and is absolutely of the best quality. It was completed in 1874.

of flaws or 'greys' in the barrel; steel does not have this disadvantage and the barrels can be made lighter and stronger. In general, it is preferable for Damascus barrels to be thick, and whilst the same is essentially true of steel barrels, they do not have to be as thick as good Damascus to offer a superior amount of strength. There are, of course, exceptions to this and a gun recently sold at Christie's bears this out. The gun was one of Lord Ripon's Purdey hammer guns and it had been rebarrelled by Purdey's, with Damascus, in 1886 following a shooting accident in which Lord Ripon had blown the tops of the barrels off as he fired his No. 3 gun. Despite being approximately 15 thousandths of an inch thick in one barrel, the gun passed a nitro reproof in 1992.

There are many earlier collectable hammer guns, the classic guide to them being Crudgington & Baker's *The British Shotgun, Vols 1 & 2*. This market revolves around interesting patents of one form or another and covers rarities such as base-fire guns in which the hammers are broad and blunt because a blow anywhere on the base of the cartridge would ignite the charge, and other more commonly encountered guns such as the needle-fire introduced by Needham about 1850. In this design, the percussion cap in the cartridge is fired by a needle-like striker and the guns can have breech blocks which swing out to be loaded. In other designs such as the Montigny system, the gun has a sliding breech action with independent plugs sliding in the breech channels, the whole being operated by a lift-up extended lever with an integral pivoted latch.

Interesting and unusual actions also revolve around the methods of fastening the barrels to the action, patents for various forms of actions and strikers and for methods of opening such as the Westley Richards 1862 patent in which the toplever is pulled back and then, in a later modification, pushed to one side. Many other guns will use one or other version of the rotary underlever, the sidelever or some other form of underlever. Purdey guns in this period, for example, incorporate a modification of the Henry Jones underlever in which the entire triggerguard becomes the lever and, on being unhooked, swings out to release the barrels – leaving the triggers unprotected.

Other Purdey opening systems use a lever which is an integral part of the triggerguard and the forward operation of the lever will release the barrels. On closing, the lever returns automatically to its previous position in a snap-action; this particular patent is encountered in two forms with a long or a short lever, the long lever being the earlier of the two.

A much rarer variant of the hammer gun than the majority of these systems is the hammer *ejector* gun which is associated with the very end of the development of the centre fire hammer gun. As these guns were used well into the hammerless period, particularly by some of the greatest shots of the age, it is not surprising that the latest developments such as ejectors were also incorporated in the guns. Some hammer guns, therefore, were built as hammer ejector guns whilst others were converted to ejector at a later date. The makers of such guns were almost invariably the best names of the age and the majority of true hammer ejector guns in existence today were built by Purdey and Boss.

Hammer guns were not easily removed by the new hammerless designs. Whilst Daw's introduction of the centre-fire cartridge in 1861 and subsequent early hammerless designs such as Murcott's 'Mousetrap' of 1871 were the precursors of

today's gun, people, as in the flintlock and percussion ages that had gone before, were reluctant to put aside those things that were familiar. Many sportsmen, for example, felt unhappy with hammerless guns because they couldn't actually *see* whether they were cocked or not; hence the development of early 'tell-tales' such as crystal panels which gave visual access to the inner workings of the hammerless gun.

Gradually, however, new concepts eased their way into acceptance. With the exception of certain patents which had introduced self-cocking or self half-cocking for hammer guns, the external hammers of such guns had always to be drawn back to full cock by hand; with hammerless guns, however, the work of cocking the internal hammers or tumblers was done on the fall or closure of the barrels. The introduction of further mechanisms such as Needham's ejector patent of 1874 meant that cartridges no longer had to be plucked by hand from the chambers, and in time, with various forms of intercepting safeties which served to calm the fears of the newly-converted, the hammerless gun came into its own.

There are a number of early hammerless designs that should be of interest to a collector of English sporting guns and there are any number of variations on the principles mentioned above. I have already mentioned Crudgington & Baker's *The British Shotgun, Vol. 1* as probably the best guide of its type to the intricacies of all the various patents and *Vol. 2* covers the early hammerless period in much the same style. For our purposes, this section ends with the final development of the sidelock and the Anson & Deeley boxlock as the two major, fully-developed expressions of the modern English gun.

A rare Boss patent 12-bore hammer ejector gun, No. 4147. The gun was built *circa* 1891 and the ejector patent claimed is probably No. 11623 of 1887, granted to Henry William Holland (of Holland & Holland) and John Robertson (who became a partner in Boss & Co. in 1891).

5

Sporting Rifles

Perhaps the greatest exposition of the best English gun is the double rifle. In the heyday of the British Empire, these rifles were used for every conceivable type of hunting, whether in pursuit of big game or for soft-skinned quarry such as boar and antelope. The double rifle configuration provides the most efficient and effective combination of speed and reliability in the discharge of two well-aimed shots that is to be had. It is therefore not surprising that such rifles were absolutely *de riguer* for any type of African or Indian hunting and they will be found in a considerable array of calibres.

The British experience of hunting in all climates and under all conditions was passed directly back to the gunmakers who were asked to produce double rifles for use against the most dangerous animals under the most adverse circumstances, and their production extended through to any number of smaller bore rifles for plains game or lighter quarry. The most desirable collectable calibre remains the .600 of which only a very limited number were made. The .600 was, at one time, the most powerful commercial rifle cartridge in the world, generating a devastating 7600 fps muzzle energy with a 900 grain bullet, and with only a few cheaper exceptions, it was built to the most exacting standards. Such rifles weigh at least 16 lb and have massive actions and breech-ends. The barrels are invariably built on chopper lumps and such is the strength required at the radius of the action that side bolsters are also usually added to the actions. Further strengthening to the hands of the stocks is provided by elongated top straps which extend back from the action body to cover the comb of the stock and the safeties are usually, but not always, manual. The argument for a manual safe in a rifle designed for dangerous game is quite simple: a hunter might find

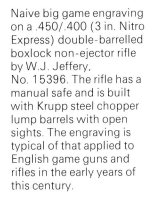

Naive big game engraving on a .450/.400 (3 in. Nitro Express) double-barrelled boxlock non-ejector rifle by W.J. Jeffery, No. 15396. The rifle has a manual safe and is built with Krupp steel chopper lump barrels with open sights. The engraving is typical of that applied to English game guns and rifles in the early years of this century.

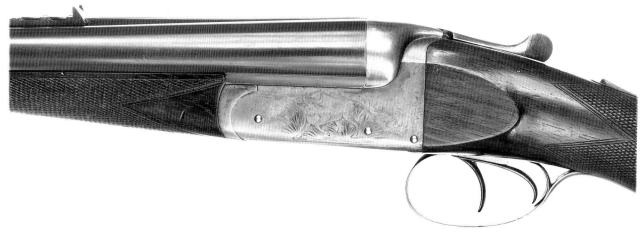

J. Woodward .303 'The Automatic' double-barrelled sidelock non-ejector rifle No. 5383. Note the arcaded or 'umbrella' fences and the protruding tumbler pivots with their gold inlaid cocking indicators; both are typical Woodward features, as is the close foliate-scroll engraving. Of interest too are the bolted safety, the side clips and the snap action under lever.

himself under considerable pressure from a charging animal and having a safe that does not return to 'safe' after the opening of the barrels gives one less thing to divert his attention. Any safe will also make a small 'click' as it is pushed on and it is therefore desirable to minimize any disturbance when stalking game at close quarters.

The short, heavy barrels on a .600 will also usually be complemented by a sturdy, thickset stock with a pistol grip (for added grip), a cheek piece and a good recoil pad of the most classic type, usually a Silvers rubber pad covered with pigskin. The .600 was very much the ultimate expression of English gunmaking skills, and it is therefore common to find them engraved or embellished in ways that befitted their exalted status. Rifles built for the Indian Maharajas, for example, were often inlaid or damascened with gold and they might also have precious stones added as foresights; the .600/.577 double rifle built by Holland & Holland for the Maharajah of Rewa, for example, has a diamond as a foresight. Others, particularly those of modern construction will have special engraving of big game scenes but there are others which will have standard engraving motifs that are simply exquisitely executed.

I have said that such rifles are rare and I am certain that no more than one, and perhaps two, have appeared on the public market in recent decades. A collector might need, therefore, to concentrate on slightly smaller calibres but even here, with rifles built in calibres such as the .577, .500/.465 and .470 Nitro Express, the availability is limited and when they do appear for sale they are quickly sold, whatever their condition. The .577 (3 in.) Nitro Express cartridge was one of the most popular African calibres; it was used, as was the .600, as a necessary stand-by for any type of big game in the most difficult of circumstance and, with its 7010 fps muzzle energy combined with a 790 grain bullet, it was reckoned by some to be even more effective than a double .600, particularly in terms of its penetrative capacity.

In addition to these two very large calibres, there is now a particular preference for two big game calibres both of which possess the ideal combination of a comfortable weight with a medium size cartridge developing excellent ballistics. These are the .470 Nitro Express and the .375 (H&H) Belted Rimless Magnum; rifles built in these calibres are just about the most sought-after with, of course,

(*This page and opposite*) A selection of best English stalking rifles all built on classic Mauser action: (*left*) .375 (H. & H. Belted Rimless Magnum) by Holland & Holland, No. 3625, *circa* 1974; (*right*) .244 (H. & H. Magnum) by Holland & Holland, No. 3071, *circa* 1970

(*left*) 7 × 57 mm by Mauser, No. 60858,
without any English finishing; (*centre*) .303
by J. Rigby, No. 4132, *circa* 1913; (*right*)
.275 by J. Rigby, No. 3323, *circa* 1909.

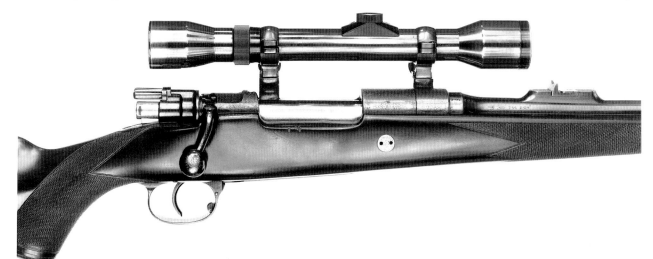

One of a very limited number of stalking rifles built by Purdey's, this 7 mm Mauser sporting rifle, No. 25927, was built in 1955 and was finished with fine rose and scroll engraving.

the exception of the very rare types. Rifles in both these calibres have been produced by many makers, but today the .470 is very much associated with the famous rifle-makers John Rigby & Co. and a best rifle by this maker is a very desirable collector's piece indeed. Such rifles are characterised by fluted fences, dipped-edge lockplates and actions which incorporate the Rigby-Bissell patent in which a rising bolt in the action 'detonating' secures a horseshoe-shaped extension to the barrels. The .375 Belted Rimless Magnum cartridge was introduced by Holland & Holland in 1912 and tends, therefore, to be associated with that maker. Holland & Holland 'Royal' double rifles for this and other calibres are, with the exception of Rigby's, perhaps the most famous, and their general characteristics are short lockplates with back-action mechanisms which were introduced to strengthen the rifle actions. Some others have true backlocks without any extension of the lockplate into the action bar.

It is very encouraging to find that all the leading gun and rifle makers are continuing their production of double rifles. Purdey's, for example, have recently completed .375, .470 and .600 calibre rifles and in 1988, Holland & Holland, in association with the collector William Feldstein and the American cartridge manufacturers B.E.L.L., designed and produced an entirely new .700 Nitro Express double rifle. Unlike the many 'wildcat' cartridges which are currently available in the United States and elsewhere, the .700 is an entirely original design and the production of rifles for this cartridge has given a new and much needed impetus to best gunmaking in Britain. Needless to say, such rifles are massive, and they need to be; the .700 cartridge develops a muzzle energy of 8900 fps with a 1000 grain bullet.

Westley Richards also continue their rifle-making activities; they, along with Holland & Holland, are chiefly remembered for their contribution to the creation of the Indian princely armouries and they have produced a bewildering variety of double rifles, including single trigger 'Ovundo' detachable boxlock ejector rifles and 'Fauneta' rifled-choke shot-and-bullet guns. Mention of the latter brings to mind the 'Paradox' shot-and-ball guns produced by Holland & Holland. This was a design invented by Colonel G. Vincent Fosbery, VC, and incorporates smooth bore barrels with rifled chokes. Such guns also have sights and are designed to take a spherical ball or, other lighter game permitting, shot, and were ideal for use in areas where a great mixture of game was to be had; 'Fauneta' and 'Paradox' gun/rifles are often described as 'Cape' guns.

The discussion so far has been limited to sidelock double rifles and mention should be made, finally, of Boss rifles. The Boss production of rifles, and particularly double rifles was very small, and they are consequently very much sought after. A Boss *over-and-under* double rifle must be, perhaps, the rarest of any type, including the marvellous three-barrel shotgun combinations produced chiefly by Boss and Dickson's.

We should not curtail our brief discussion of double rifles without mention of the worthy boxlock types. Such rifles were, for obvious reasons, produced in greater numbers, and a collector will, consequently, have greater choice. They were produced in all calibres, including .600, and whilst some were very highly finished indeed, with scroll-back action bodies and de luxe engraving, the majority tend to be plain, workaday rifles, designed for serious everyday use in the most remote and inhospitable hunting territories. Many will have border engraving of one sort or another; others are decorated with naive big-game scenes featuring lions, tigers and buffalo with strange or bizarre appearances – it is easy to forget that many of the craftsmen who built these rifles at, for example, the turn of the century, had no direct experience of the actual appearance of these animals and their attempts to achieve a representation are sometimes rather touching.

Mention should also be made of nineteenth-century double hammer pin-fire and centre-fire rifles. These were initially made in traditional bore sizes, such as 4, 8, 10 and 12 but later in the Black Powder era new 'Express' calibres were introduced which were to become the precursors of the later great smokeless or cordite cartridges. In general, the characteristics of hammer rifles are much the same as those of hammer shotguns but they were made with a particular preference for the Jones-type screw underlever which provided a very solid and positive method of closure – particularly for guns built to withstand the higher pressures generated by the new rifle cartridges. Such rifles are also quite often fitted with bolted safeties to the hammers and, where they have remained intact,

A .318 (W.R. Accelerated Express) double-barrelled single trigger 'Ovundo' detachable boxlock ejector rifle by Westley Richards, No. 17894, completed *circa* 1923.

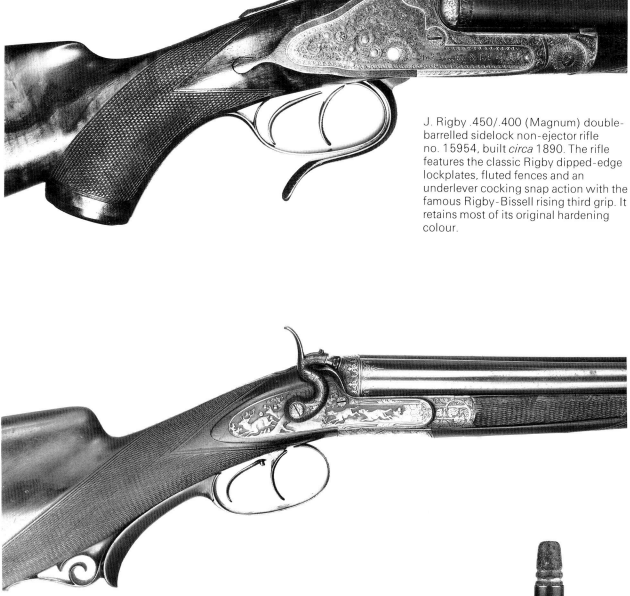

J. Rigby .450/.400 (Magnum) double-barrelled sidelock non-ejector rifle no. 15954, built *circa* 1890. The rifle features the classic Rigby dipped-edge lockplates, fluted fences and an underlever cocking snap action with the famous Rigby-Bissell rising third grip. It retains most of its original hardening colour.

Some of the most ornate rifles were built by continental makers. This 10.5 × 47 (R) mm double-barrelled rifle was built by J. Nowotny of Prague, *circa* 1880, and has exquisitely cut decoration. In keeping with the general style of European hunting rifles of the last century, it has an ornate horn triggerguard and Lefaucheux-type underlevers. The cartridge (*right*) for which it was built is now obsolete and very difficult to find.

will have beautifully built oak cases with provision for every possible type of loading accessory, including bullet and ball moulds, powder measures and finely finished turnscrews. With the exception of those makers already mentioned, hammer rifles by Alexander Henry are particularly sought after.

The mechanical problems associated with double rifles have much in common with those mentioned in a later chapter concerning shotguns. All rifles of this type are susceptible to stock and action fractures and, with the higher pressures involved, particular care should be taken when ascertaining the seriousness of any structural flaw in the action. There are, however, certain particular problems which are unique to rifles. The first concerns the 'regulating' of the shooting of the rifle, which is a very demanding art. It is common for rifles that have been stored for many years or which have been subjected to poor or careless handling or extremes of damp or temperature to loose their ability to shoot to the correct point; it therefore becomes necessary to re-regulate the rifle and this can involve the dismantling of the barrels and the building of new sight-blocks and sights. Certain makers have introduced a method in their construction of double rifle barrels in which a wedge of steel is inserted at the muzzle to help move the barrels further apart or closer together to achieve perfect shooting. The 'wedge' is subsequently finished off when the barrels are fully finished, but it will remain in place for future possible alteration. Another point of particular importance for rifles is that they are usually regulated with a particular type and manufacture of cartridge which will have specific loading and bullet characteristics. Where such cartridges become obsolete, and this is very much the case with rifle cartridges, a newer cartridge will have to be used which might well perform differently. In some cases, a rifle built for an old and completely out of date cartridge for which sufficient stocks no longer exist, will be converted

A .450 ($3\frac{1}{4}$ in.) double-barrelled hammer rifle by J. Rigby, No. 15362 with its Jones patent rotary underlever. Note also the rebounding backlocks with their bolted hammers.

to a newer and more popular cartridge. From a purist's point of view, such conversions will destroy the original nature of the rifle and in recent decades there has been a particular willingness to convert old but eminently collectable best rifles to current European cartridges such as the 9.3 × 74 (R). Whilst such rifles are assured a continuing and useful life, they become little more than a shadow of their former selves.

The other great problem concerning rifles lies in the condition of the bore itself. Whilst use is not in itself a destroyer of rifling, the incorrect cleaning and care of the barrels is, and this is so particularly where the old acidic nitro-cellulose cartridges were used. A collector will, therefore, encounter rifles that have poor bores and he should take particular care with obviously badly worn or pitted barrels. Where this is extreme, and causes the rifle to shoot badly, conversion to a different calibre, or rebarrelling, are usually the only remedies.

I will, in a later chapter, give a brief guide to proof marks for rifles and I will repeat the fundamental points here, as they are relevant. The styles of rifle markings in earlier years are not as consistent as those of shotguns and there is a greater variation in the forms of marking. Double rifles built before about 1887 will normally be marked with a bore number which will indicate the *nominal* calibre, but very often, small bore rifles will not have any bore number at all. There is a growing consistency in marking from about 1887 when particular loads were specified and from 1925 rifles are also marked with the nominal case length; from 1925, therefore, a .450 (3 in.) rifle, for example, will have proof marks specifying the powder used and the weight of the bullet in grains; prior to 1904, the marks might also include 'BALL'. Even greater consistency was introduced in 1954 when both nominal case length and service pressures in tons per square inch were introduced and, in common with shotguns, full metric marks were introduced in 1984/5.

A section on sporting rifles will also, of necessity, need to include mention of single shot rifles which can be divided, in very broad terms, into those rifles

A .303 Farquharson patent falling-block rifle by G. Gibbs, No. 18286, action use number 902, frame number 379, with a manual lever safe. The rifle was built sometime between 1894 and 1900 and was subsequently rebarrelled to .303 by J. Rigby.

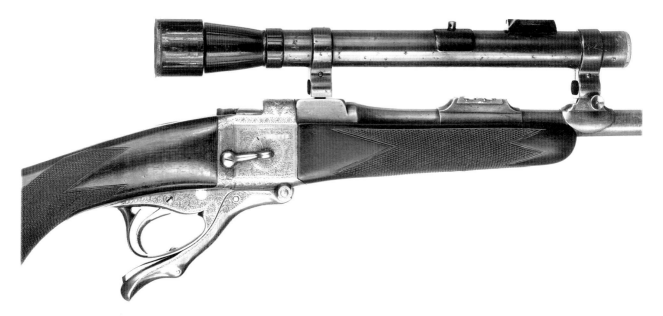

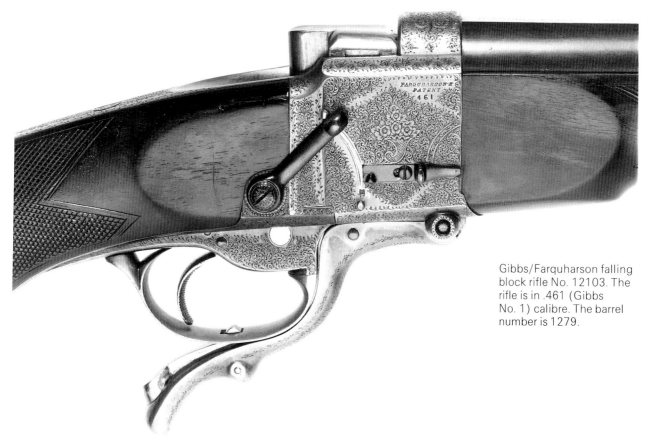

Gibbs/Farquharson falling block rifle No. 12103. The rifle is in .461 (Gibbs No. 1) calibre. The barrel number is 1279.

built on falling-block actions and those with bolt actions. There are, of course, many variations on these, but a collector should pay particular attention to best quality English falling-block rifles for which the market is particularly good. The great classic among falling-block rifles is the Gibbs-Farquharson, the mechanism of which was patented in 1872. These rifles are exquisitely built and immensely strong; the action consists of a falling-block or breech operated by an underlever and all Gibbs' rifles of this type will bear a serial number, an action use number and a frame number. The actions and furniture are usually finished with close foliate-scroll engraving and the original barrels will all have classic Metford rifling. In common with many other rifles, a good number of Gibbs-Farquharson rifles have been re-barrelled to different calibres over the years, and particular care should be taken when viewing the rifle. Later, more modern rifling, in for example, a 1910 rifle, will indicate re-barrelling as will an unusual calibre; one recent example had been converted from its original .450/400 to .280 Flanged. Sadly, the Gibbs records for their earlier production are not extensive and some were destroyed in the Second World War, but basic details are still sometimes available. Other eminently collectable falling-block rifles include the great nineteenth-century match rifles such as the Gibbs-Metford .461 rifles, some of which can still be found with their original cases, including sets of interchangeable target sights, which are of particular interest and value to collectors.

Other collectable single-shot rifles include the famous Martini-action rifles

A .250 Semi-smooth bore boxlock rook rifle by Holland & Holland, No. 24225. A characteristic Edwardian firearm, the rook rifle could only now be built at prohibitively high cost. They were, at one time, cheaply and easily available from the best makers.

but these tend to be plainer and cheaper and they are not as desirable unless highly finished. There are also Winchesters which present an entirely self-contained world which requires a highly specialized knowledge to navigate. Needless to say, some Winchesters, particularly the 1 of 100 and 1 of 1000 variants and those with special finishes or provenances, command exceptional prices. In March 1993, one of Annie Oakley's Winchesters was sold at Christie's and it achieved the astonishing price of £84,000. It did, however, have the three most desirable features, the possession of which will ensure a spectacular price. In the first instance, it had been specially built for Annie Oakley and it was subsequently used by her in many circus appearances. In the second instance, it was, in itself, a considerable rarity; it was built as a smoothbore rifle to enable Annie to fire dust-shot cartridges. Whilst the term 'smoothbore rifle' might appear to some to be a contradiction in terms, it is precisely what it says – a Winchester with Winchester rifle characteristics, but supplied at the factory in 1888, with a smoothbore barrel. The last feature in this tremendous sale was the provenance. The rifle had been presented by Annie to the grandfather of the present owner and it had been in the possession of the family ever since.

Our last thoughts concerning sporting rifles should be for bolt-action rifles. With the exception of the many military examples available and for which this book has no scope, the two most collectable types are, in order of importance, the Mauser and the Mannlicher Schoenauer. Mauser rifles were captured in their hundreds of thousands at the end of the First World War and British gunmakers

J. Rigby .300 (.295) boxlock rook rifle, No. 9924, built in the 1880s.

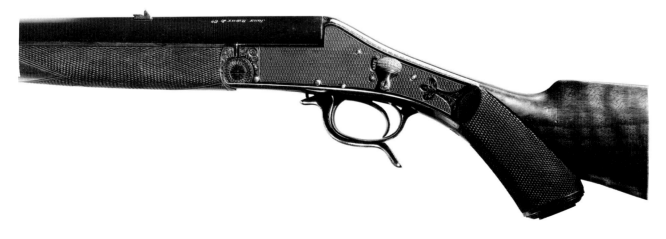

were quick to capitalize on this huge supply of one of the strongest and most reliable rifle actions ever built. Consequently, many Mauser '98 actions were used as the basis for British sporting rifles and large numbers were produced, particularly at Rigby's, in a great number of calibres. The calibre most often encountered, however, is the .275 which became, perhaps, the greatest classic stalking cartridge in the world, but others, particularly the big game calibres were built on the highly prized magnum Mauser actions. The appearance of the two – the standard and the magnum – is very much the same, but the magnum action can be identified fairly readily by its greater length and by the occasional addition of a two or three stage receiver ring. The Mannlicher Schoenauer action has a smoother action than the Mauser but it is not as desirable. In general, Mannlichers are restricted to the 6.5 mm and 8 mm calibres, and whilst they have also become classics of design, they are somewhat more limited in their appeal.

Our discussion of collectable sporting rifles ends with the smallest – the rook rifle. These were made in large numbers by virtually all British gunmakers and they were designed specifically for rook and vermin shooting. The calibres usually encountered are .295 and .300 and some can have an unusually high degree of finish. In general, however, the rook rifles encountered nowadays have suffered neglect and the bores are usually pitted; others are sometimes converted to .410 smoothbore and thereby loose much of their collectability, but the few that remain in good condition will command a premium, especially if they are by one of our more famous makers.

A .455 Webley Fosbery patent Model 1901 recoil-operated revolver, No. 708, retailed by J. MacNaughton and supplied with a shorter than normal 4 in. barrel.

No section of this type would be complete without some mention of pistols, however brief. Unfortunately for our purposes, most pistols, whether automatic or revolver, have been built for essentially military purposes. There is, however, considerable appeal in these weapons and many leading collections have some basis in the selection of good examples of the most desirable types. We find, therefore, good numbers of Luger and Mauser automatic pistols and Colt and Smith & Wesson revolvers and there are many rare variants of each type to interest a collector. The rare Borchardt 1893 Patent 7.65 mm self-loading pistol, for example, was an early precursor of the Luger; it was invented by Hugo Borchardt, a German emigrant to America who had worked for Winchester and Sharps. He returned

A rare 7.63 mm Mauser 'Large Ring Transitional' Model 1896 self-loading carbine pistol, No. 120, retailed by Westley Richards with its leather holster and associated shoulder stock.

A cased .455 Webley-Kaufmann double action revolver, No. 627, retailed by the Army & Navy Stores. An important precursor of subsequent Webley Government contract models, the Webley-Kaufmann arose from the partnership of the inventor Michael Kaufmann with Webleys in the years 1878 to 1881. This particular example is unusual in retaining almost all its original nickel-plated finish. The original lined and fitted oak case is another important collectable feature.

PLATE 11 (*above*) A set of three 'Regal XXV' boxlock ejector guns by Churchill, in 20, 28 and .410 (3 in.) bore, No. 23813/4/5/. Note the gold inlaid XXV on the breech ends of the barrels – Churchill's trademark for 25 in. barrels of which he was the greatest exponent. (*below*) The trigger plate action of a Dickson Round Action ejector gun, No. 7286. The gun was completed *circa* 1934 and the mechanism is fully gold washed and colour hardened.

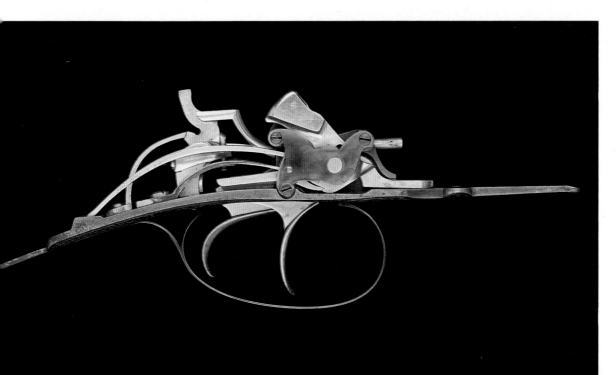

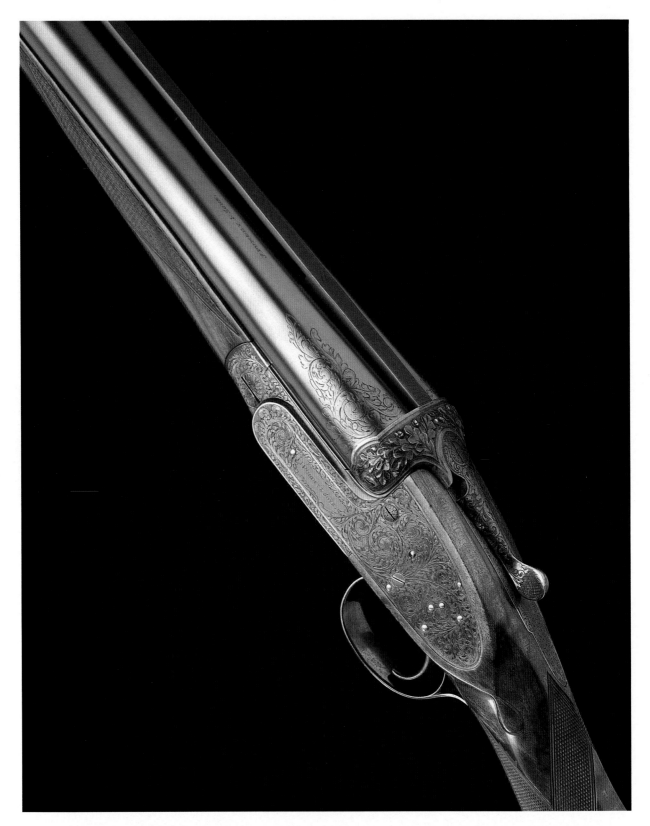

PLATE 12   A 12-bore (2¾ in.) single-trigger self-opening sidelock ejector live pigeon gun by J. Purdey, No. 26699, built in 1957 for professional competition shooting and supplied with a set of extra barrels. The engraving and embellishment is of the very highest standard. Note also the absence of a 'safe' which, together with a single trigger firing reverse barrel order (left-right) is very much a feature of live pigeon guns.

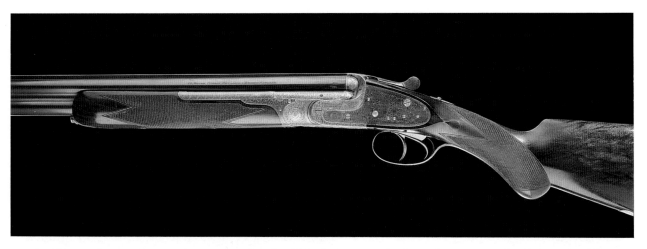

PLATE 13 *(above)* A rare 28-bore over-and-under sidelock ejector gun by Boss, No. 7254, completed *circa* 1925. The gun is one of no more than about eight built by this maker. *(below)* A magnificent set of Prussian de luxe engraved presentation guns by J.P. Sauer, in 20, 16, 12 and 10 bore. The guns bear German pre-war proof marks and were probably built between 1910 and 1925.

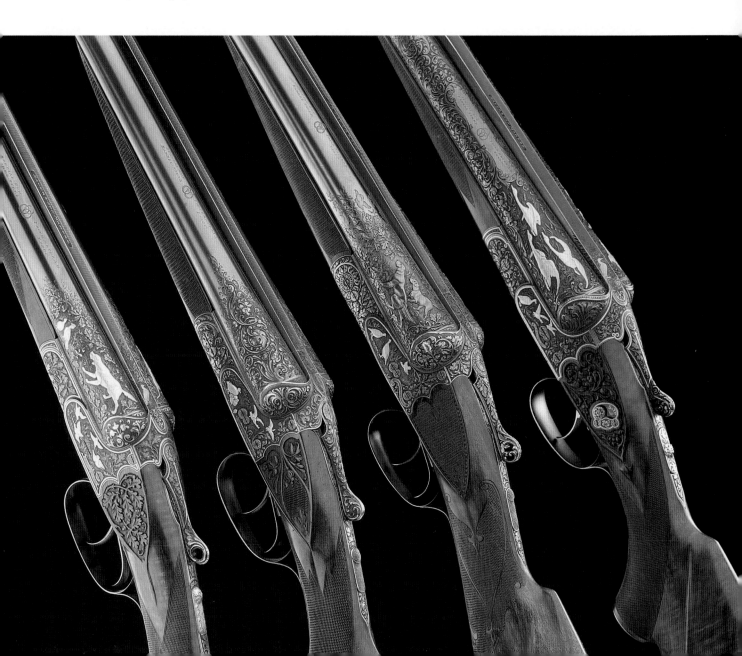

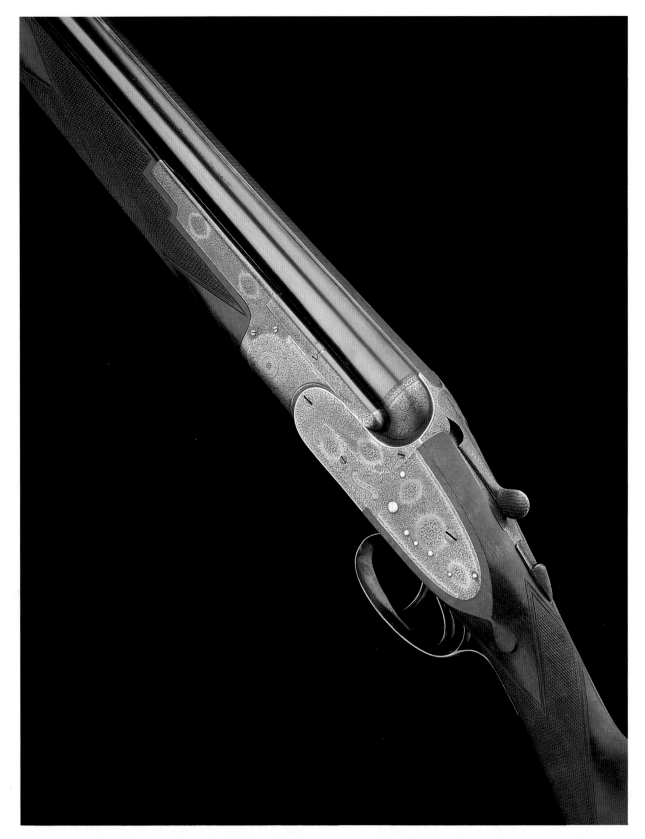

PLATE 14   Boss 12-bore (2¾ in.) over-and-under sidelock ejector gun No. 5836, completed *circa* 1910.

to Germany in the mid-1880s where he joined Ludwig Loewe & Co. of Berlin and introduced his design which was revolutionary in the successful combination of recoil operation and the so-called toggle-lock in a handgun, and in the efficiency of its operation.

It has been estimated that a little over a thousand Borchardt pistols were built by Ludwig Loewe & Co. before the company was succeeded by D.W.M. in 1896. The pistols were built to extremely high standards using the best possible materials and were advertised extensively in Britain and America where they were offered 'complete with three extra Magazines, Tools, Oilers, Holster, and Straps' at $30 (the case was $5 extra). Such complete sets, including the original case, accessories and instruction manuals are very highly-prized collector's items and will command high prices at auction.

Other rarities include Mauser carbines, and revolvers such as the Webley Fosbery Patent Model 1901 recoil-operated revolver which achieved considerable fame as a robust and accurate target and military pistol. Mention should also be made of the Webley 'W.G.' target revolver for which there is a good and consistent collector's market. Such beautifully made objects are the enduring record of a past age.

Two great classics: a .455 Webley Fosbery revolver, No. 441 and a 7.63 Mauser Model 1896 self-loading pistol, No. 51402. They are almost exactly contemporary.

6

Accessories

A .500 (No. 2 Express) double-barrelled hammer rifle by J. Rigby, No. 14663, with its full complement of accessories. Such complete, cased items are increasingly hard to find – the accessories are inevitably the first items to be mislaid.

With few exceptions, accessories are designed to be used and they will, therefore, be encountered as often on the shooting field as in a collection. Chief among these accessories are gun cases and cartridge magazines. The quality of both types will vary considerably, but again, the older the case, the more likely it is to be of excellent quality. Oak and leather double and single cases by the most famous makers are the most highly prized, with the rather more unusual triple cases for sets of three guns having a smaller but equally buoyant market. True oak and leather cases are built on a solid oak frame and they are finished with high quality locks and brass corners. There are other types which have a simple oak-lined base, but these are not generally as nice. Nineteenth-century hammer gun cases will frequently have tooled leather exteriors and fully-fitted interiors, with leather-covered compartments for the stock, action and barrels, the forend and for all manner of loading accessories, including shot and powder measures and, for rifles, bullet moulds. Both double and single gun cases will come in two classic styles: as 'flat' cases in which case they will be either of oak and leather or leather; and as 'motor' cases in which they are of a more upright, rectangular shape. Motor cases are not constructed of oak and leather, the design lending itself to the construction of lighter weight cases and being composed, therefore, of leather over a lighter wood frame. Motor case designs for double guns also come in two styles. In the first and most commonly encountered instance, the case is undivided, the stocks and actions being placed at the bottom of the case, with the barrels above. In this design, *both*

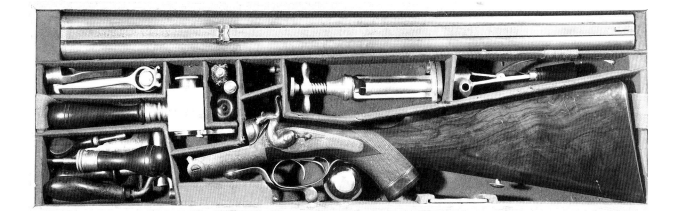

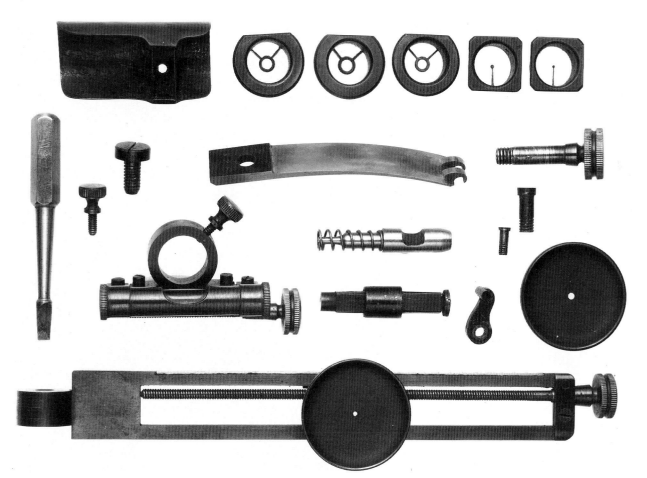

sets of barrels should be removed before attempting to take out either of the stocks and actions; leaving one set of barrels in while attempting to remove a stock and action might lead to small dents to the barrels or scratches to the barrel blueing. The second design, which was used almost exclusively by Boss, Woodward and Churchill has two entirely separate compartments, one for each gun, thereby eliminating the problem described above.

Oak and leather cases, tend, for obvious reasons, to be heavy, and whilst many people like to have a case of this type for display purposes, they will also sometimes want a lighter case for everyday use. Some pairs of guns, therefore, will come with a normal oak and leather double case and a lightweight single case for use when one or other of the guns is being used independently. Many makers produced lightweight leather or canvas cases, but the type most often encountered is the Churchill 'V.C.' case, a very compact variant in which the 'toe' of the stock tucks up beneath the barrel compartment, thereby reducing the necessary width of the case. Finally, some makers, particularly Greener and Dickson, produced de luxe cases with velvet-lined interiors, gold-tooled leather trade labels and interior flaps. Others, and this is more common with modern presentation guns by Holland & Holland, have produced marvellously inlaid wooden cases with all manner of added features and refinements.

Cartridge magazines are also highly collectable. Again, the most desirable are

A cased set of orthoptic sights for G. Gibbs .461 (Gibbs No. 1) Farquharson/Mitford patent falling block match rifle No. 14159 (action No. 537, barrel No. 1406). The set comprises a supine backsight with an aperture disc, an adjustable frontsight with five elements, spirit level and windage scale, and miscellaneous other accessories including a spare striker. The case lid is inscribed in gilt letters 'Metford Rifle Sights/ G. Gibbs, Bristol'.

(*This page and opposite*) Five of the most popular
types of gun case label.

The Bombay Armoury cartridge board showing a comprehensive selection of Eley & Kynoch cartridges.

brass-mounted oak and leather magazines by makers such as Purdey, Holland & Holland and Boss. The best magazines are true oak and leather cases, with internal leather straps and removable partitions. One example recently encountered was by Churchill and had provision for 2 in., $2\frac{1}{2}$ in. and $2\frac{3}{4}$ in. cartridges; a slight alteration in the positioning of the internal partitions resulted in wider or narrower sections for the cartridges. Cartridge magazines built for more than about 300 cartridges tend to be exceptionally heavy and the most popular in terms of size, therefore, tend to be those for 150 to 250 cartridges. The modern cost of these cases has meant that many buyers are now concentrating on older, secondhand cases; as with gun cases, there seems to be a general preference for those cases with a certain amount of wear and tear and with some 'age'. There is also a general recognition of the excellent quality of many of these vintage accessories, and if they come with a number of interesting steamer and hotel labels from the twenties and thirties, so much the better.

Cartridge display cases are visually dramatic accessories; they were supplied to the English trade by cartridge and munitions manufacturers such as Eley, Kynoch and Nobel, as selections from their current productions of sporting and military cartridges. Many were shipped abroad to the colonies and it is still possible to find display boards with the names of the original retailers. One such was a board supplied to the Bombay Armoury, illustrating a variety of Eley and Kynoch cartridges and components. In common with the general style of these display boards, the cartridges were radially arranged around a central Nobel card, and the selection comprised 172 centre-fire brass-case rifle and pistol cartridges in various calibres including what was then the most powerful big

Two Eley cartridge boards illustrating a number of rifle and shotgun cartridges. The amount displayed is a fraction of the production during the heyday of the best English guns.

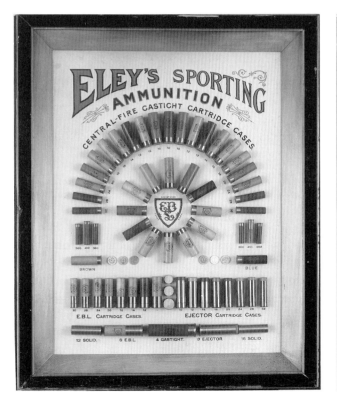

game cartridge in the world, the .600 Nitro Express, and seventy centre-fire paper-case shot cartridges of various brands, including Acme, Bonax, Kyblack, Primax, Sporting Ballistite, Velocity and Westminster, in gauges 12 to .410. There were also 35 assorted rim-fire cartridges and twelve tins of components and sundry top-cards, the whole being mounted on maroon baize. The case was oak framed and glazed and it measured 48 in. by 39 in. overall. This was, by any standards, a large board; the most commonly encountered size is about 31 in. by 25 in. or 20 in. overall and the selections tend to be smaller. The most popular boards will have a good selection of big-game rifle cartridges, including the .600 Nitro Express, .577, .500/.465, .470 and .375 Magnum, and will have a wide selection of vintage shotgun cartridges. The addition of one or two rarities, such as Eley's Rocket cartridge will make them even more interesting. There

A leather, brass and steel McArthur and Prain 1905 patent 'Gannochy Rapid Load' cartridge dispenser, with tooled exterior, drop-down lid and fabric inner rain flap, for one hundred 12-bore cartridges. Such cases were also supplied with interchangeable metal inner frames.

are also modern cartridge display cases but these tend to be smaller and more utilitarian in appearance. Imperial Metal Industries Ltd have produced a number of cartridge boards with an assortment of metallic and dummy cartridges, featuring a selection of modern shotgun cartridges such as Alphamax, Fourlong, Grand Prix, Gastight, Maximum, Impax, Winchester Cannon, Rifled Slug and Trapshooting. Other boards have been produced which illustrate the manufacture of, for example, an Eley 'Grand Prix' cartridge and these feature attractive cut-aways showing the composition of the cartridge.

A collector of shooting accessories might also wish to consider cartridge dispensers. A number of designs for 'rapid loaders' have been patented over the years and one of the most popular designs is the 'Gannochy' which takes its name from the Scottish estate where one of the patentees was the head keeper. The design stems from F. Vetterli's British Patent No. 4808 of 1881 in which cartridges were arranged at different levels to effect easy removal. The Gannochy is worn slung over the shoulder and offers, when opened, ten rows of cartridges with their bases outwards. The interior of the case has an aluminium square frame which supports ten rows of steel spring clips to hold the cartridges; to facilitate their withdrawal, every other row of cartridges stands proud of the adjacent row. Gannochy dispensers normally have a leather exterior with a tooled lid, a fabric inner rain-flap and they are designed to take one hundred cartridges.

Stand selectors or place finders are another interesting area for the collector. The most prized sets are by makers such as Asprey's and they will sometimes be made of gold, silver or platinum. Some come in the form of a small cylinder in which the turning of

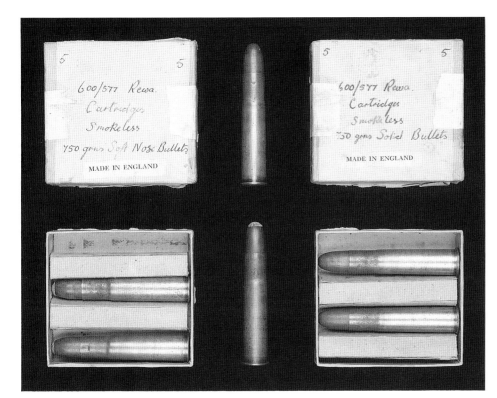

Rare sporting cartridges: six rounds of .577 Rewa both soft and solid point. The exceptional nature of this cartridge, a .600 necked down to .577, is attested by the hand-labelled boxes. The cartridges were designed for a unique Holland & Holland rifle built for His Highness Martand Singh, Maharajah of Rewa, sometime before 1929.

the base raises and rotates the markers which then face out to be selected, while others are shaped as small antique matchboxes and flasks. Other versions can be made in the form of leather pouches with ivory pegs or markers and there are, of course, other designs, such as the one in which each place number is marked on the base of a series of small silver drinking tumblers. Collectors might also like to consider game counters such as the two that sold recently at auction. The first was unusual in that it was inscribed in both English and French and it had dials for partridge, rabbits, hares and pheasants. The second was also of brass, but without any of the usual nickel-plating and it had six dials, three on each side, with provision for pheasants, grouse, partridge, hares, rabbits and woodcock. Both of these counters, or 'Norfolk Liars', as they are sometimes called, were designed to be suspended from a chain, but there are other versions which are intended to be let in to the stock of a gun. One such had two scoring wheels, numbered in tens and units, operated by a sliding thumb piece.

Other areas to consider include shot cartridge mirror boards, such as the ones produced by Kynoch in much the same way as they produced cartridge boards. These mirrors are usually bevelled and oak framed and are colourfully illustrated with a range of proprietary cartridges such as Primax, Bonax, Grouse, Opex, Kynoid, Perfectly Gastight, C.B. and Swift. Consideration should also be given to shot and powder measures, ivory and horn-handled turnscrews, specially produced snap caps, cartridge-loading combination tools, presentation gun-cleaning kits, and cartridges and cartridge boxes of which there are a great number and variety. There are also cartridge loading sets, such as the one sold by Gallyon's in 1982. Gallyon's Cambridge loading room had, at one time, produced 15,000

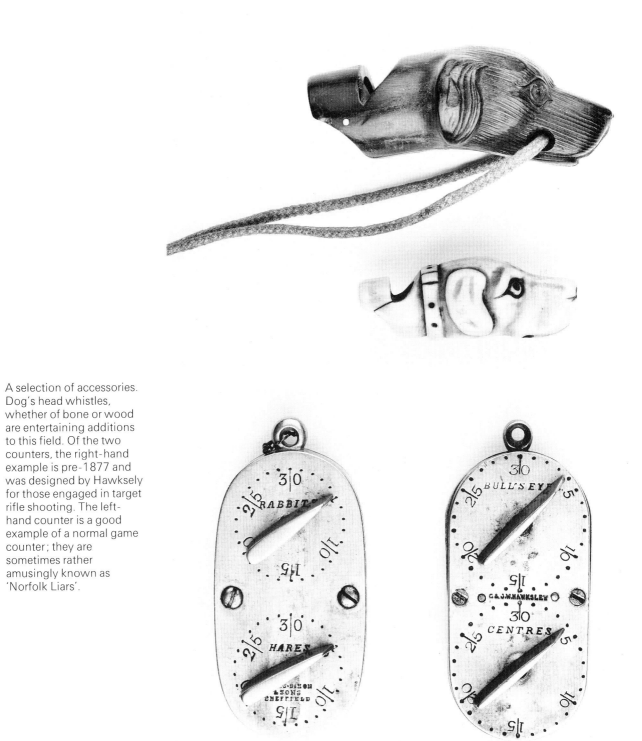

A selection of accessories. Dog's head whistles, whether of bone or wood are entertaining additions to this field. Of the two counters, the right-hand example is pre-1877 and was designed by Hawksely for those engaged in target rifle shooting. The left-hand counter is a good example of a normal game counter; they are sometimes rather amusingly known as 'Norfolk Liars'.

cartridges weekly and Gallyon's held the Royal Warrant as Cartridge Makers to Her Majesty The Queen, supplying large numbers of cartridges to Sandringham. The set comprised a Dixon 'Climax' loading machine composed of a 10-gang powdering machine, a 10-gang ramming machine, three mahogany-framed brass cartridge trays each with a brass wad tray of 100 cases, a japanned shot tray and other associated Dixon, Erskine and other loading equipment in various gauges including a tensile gauge for testing cartridge closures and various loading parts, tools and instruction booklets. Such sets are still to be found today, their bulk and heaviness acting as something of a deterrent to the 'incidental' collector.

Sporting books form a perfectly self-contained and particularly fascinating area. In general, the most highly prized are first edition copies of famous works such as Burrard's *The Modern Shotgun*, Greener's *The Breechloader* and Churchill's various works on the art of shooting. There is also a growing interest in wildfowling classics, such as the works of Wentworth Day and Stanley Duncan

A Kynoch cartridge display mirror.

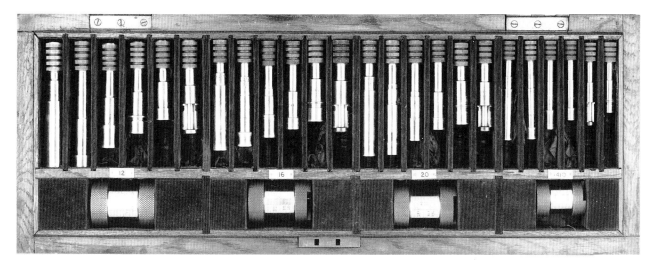

A rare set of gunmaker's
master pattern chamber
gauges, possibly made by
Charles Osborne & Co. in
the 1920s.

A Bogardus ball-trap with its necked ball targets of blue-
tinted glass containing black feathers. Targets such as these
were the forerunners of modern 'clay pigeons'; a successful
shot would produce a shower of glass and feathers.

but the highest prices are usually reserved for obscure and long out-of-print works on big game hunting in the days of the Empire. To my mind, this is possibly the most interesting area for it covers all aspects of hunting life, from Patterson's *The Man-Eaters of Tsavo* and Taylor's *Big Game and Big Game Rifles* to Maxwell's *Stalking Big Game with a Camera in Equatorial Africa*. It is also the record of a lost era.

Finally, our collector might also like to consider antique clay-pigeon traps and their associated glass ball targets such as the Bussey patent 'Gyro' trap which fired painted sheet-iron 'birds' of figure eight form; it is occasionally possible to encounter 'Bogardus'-type traps which have a coil-sprung throwing arm mounted on a pivoted board. Such traps were used to fire glass ball targets, some of which are highly interesting, with their decorative, moulded exteriors and feather-filled interiors.

Books can form one of the most interesting areas for a collector; books on the big game animals of India and Africa are, in general, the most desirable.

7

Problems

The most commonly encountered problem, in addition to material and structural flaws in the gun, is the question of 'proof'. Few people understand the terms, and fewer still know how proof is conducted and how past 'material' alterations to the barrels will have affected the original proof of the gun. The Worshipful Company of Gunmakers of the City of London and The Guardians of the Birmingham Proof House have, together, produced a small booklet which provides a concise guide to the history of proof and the regulations governing it, and which also gives illustrated examples of most internationally (C.I.P.) recognized proof marks.

The Gunmaker's Company of London was granted its Royal Charter *circa* 1637 and proof was introduced at that time to protect the public against unscrupulous gunmakers. Proof is essentially the compulsory and statutory testing of every new shotgun or small arm, and it involves firing a charge through the barrel that is substantially heavier than those found in standard cartridges; this is intended to reveal any weakness in the gun and it is carried out in two stages – provisional proof which applies to shotgun barrels in an early stage of manufacture, and definitive proof which applies to all arms. There are other 'special' proofs which deal normally with unusually heavy loads. Reproof, or the further test of a gun after its original proof, may be necessary where there is an indication of material weakness, or weakening and where there has been a significant enlargement of the internal diameter of the barrel so that it no longer conforms with the existing proof marks. There are other conditions under which reproof has to be carried out; these can include, amongst others, rebarrelling, conversion to ejector and conversion from Black Powder proof to nitro proof.

The proof process also involves stamping the barrels with a series of marks to show that the gun has been tested and that it has passed the 'provisional',

The barrels of Greener gun No. 31860 showing the first 1875 'Not for Ball' proof on the tubes and the subsequent re-proof marks on the flats.

The barrel flats of J. Dickson Round Action ejector gun No. 6449. The London proof marks are of the 1904 type. Note also the junction line of the chopper lumps along the barrel lumps.

'definitive' and 'view' stages. The marks on shotguns proved in recent years will also include a *nominal* bore size, the chamber length and the maximum service pressures for the gun. There are, however, several quite distinct patterns of shotgun proof marks, some of which will not include all, or any, of the marks mentioned above. These patterns are a very helpful guide to the age of a gun. For example, guns built prior to 1855 will bear simply the London or Birmingham proof and view marks and sometimes a bore size. Those proved after 1855, when the provisional proof mark was introduced, will bear the provisional, definitive and view marks and the bore size of the gun will be stamped twice – indicating the provisional and actual bore sizes. The requirement to mark the provisional bore sizes was dropped in 1868 and the marks from that year consist of the provisional, definitive and view marks accompanied by the bore size which will, accordingly, be marked once only. One of the most distinctive variations in marking is that introduced in 1875 when guns are found to be marked 'Not For Ball' which denotes choked barrels. The nominal chamber mark – a diamond – containing also the nominal bore size was introduced in 1887 as also was the subdivision of bore-sizes (e.g., 13/1, 8/1, 12/1). The nitro proof mark will not be found in this period but the *specific* powder for the gun will be. The year 1896 saw the introduction of another highly distinctive mark – the official 'Nitro Proof' followed by the maximum service load of shot and the word 'MAXIMUM'. The MAXIMUM marking was dropped in 1904 and the 1896 rules therefore provide us with a very clear and concise method of dating guns built or proved between 1896 and 1904. The nominal chamber length of the gun was introduced in 1925 – (e.g., $2\frac{1}{2}$, $2\frac{3}{4}$) – and the 1954 rules saw the introduction of the nominal bore size stated as an Imperial diameter (e.g., .729, .740) and the maximum service load marking was dropped in favour of the maximum service *pressure* marking (e.g., $3\frac{1}{2}$ TONS). New metric marks were introduced

Woodward gun No. 6800, built 1927. The barrel flats show the original 1925 proof marks and the later 1994 reproof marks. Note also the line between the two barrel lumps which shows the junction of the chopper lumps.

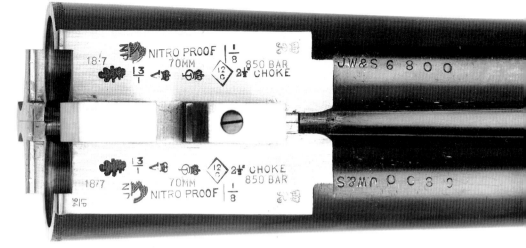

The barrel flats of Holland & Holland 'Royal' sidelock ejector gun No. 30535, built *circa* 1934. Later rebarrelling is indicated by the 1954 proof marks.

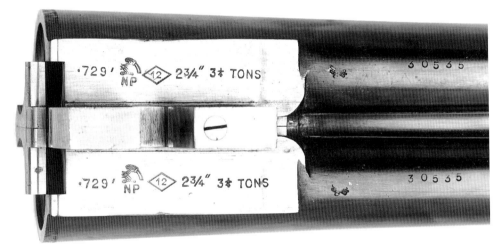

Grant 'Lightweight' assisted-opening sidelock ejector gun No. 17909 was completed *circa* 1960 but was started much earlier, in the 1930s – hence the 1925 proof marks.

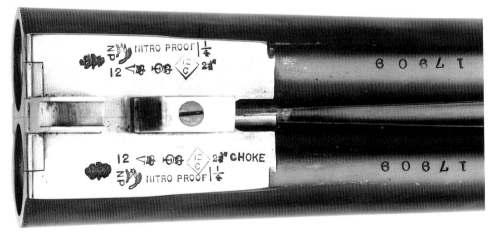

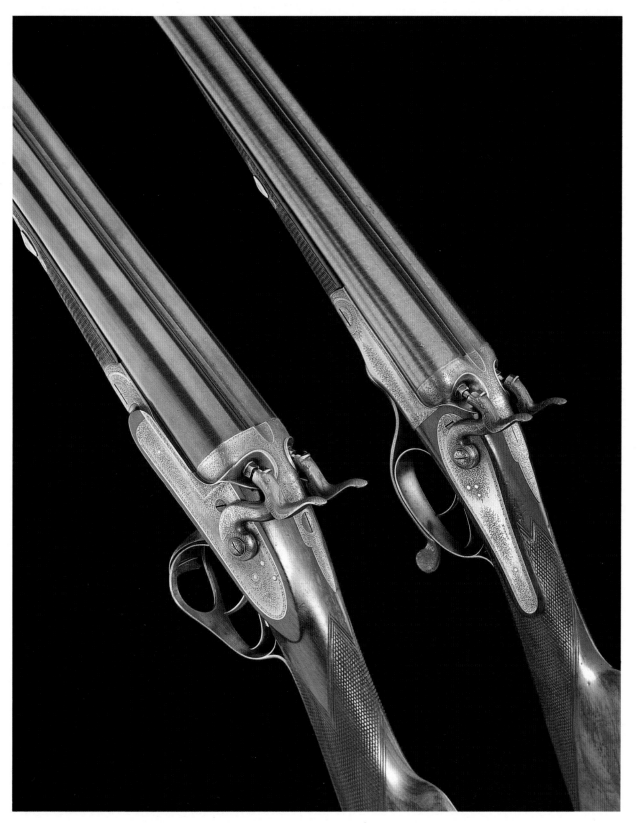

PLATE 15   A comparison of two Purdey hammer guns, both in exceptional condition for their age. The first, No. 9430 *(left)*, was completed *circa* 1875 and incorporates the Second Pattern thumb-hole underlever. The second, No. 8417 *(right)*, was built *circa* 1871 and is supplied with a Jones patent rotary underlever. Both retain traces of their original colour hardening – a remarkable achievement for guns over one hundred years old.

PLATE 16 A rare three-barrel, two-trigger, 16-bore round action ejector gun by J. Dickson, No. 4801. The Dickson & Murray patent (No. 873 of 1882) provided for three arrangements of the barrels: three-in-line (as here), one over two and two over one. Of the known examples, some have three triggers, others two, but no patent has been identified for the repeating trigger (in this case the front trigger firing the centre and right barrels), which is, in effect, a single trigger (something relatively rare in Dickson two-barrel guns). It is understood that Dickson's built 27 three-barrel guns but other examples have come to light including Nos. 3727, 3933, 4415 and 4889. No. 4801 was built in 1896 as the No. 1 of a pair.

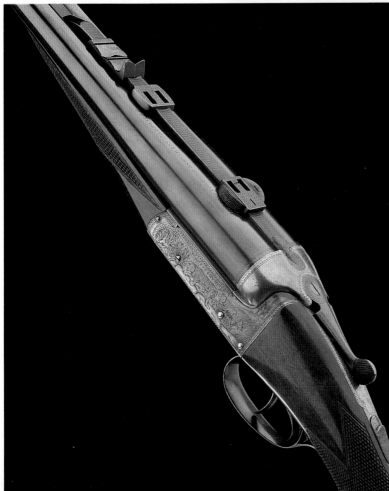

PLATE 17 *(above)* A .240 (Flanged) 'Royal' double-barrelled sidelock ejector rifle by Holland & Holland, No. 28598, completed *circa* 1924. *(left)* A .375 (H & H Belted Rimless Magnum) double-barrelled boxlock ejector rifle by W. J. Jeffery, No. 28962.

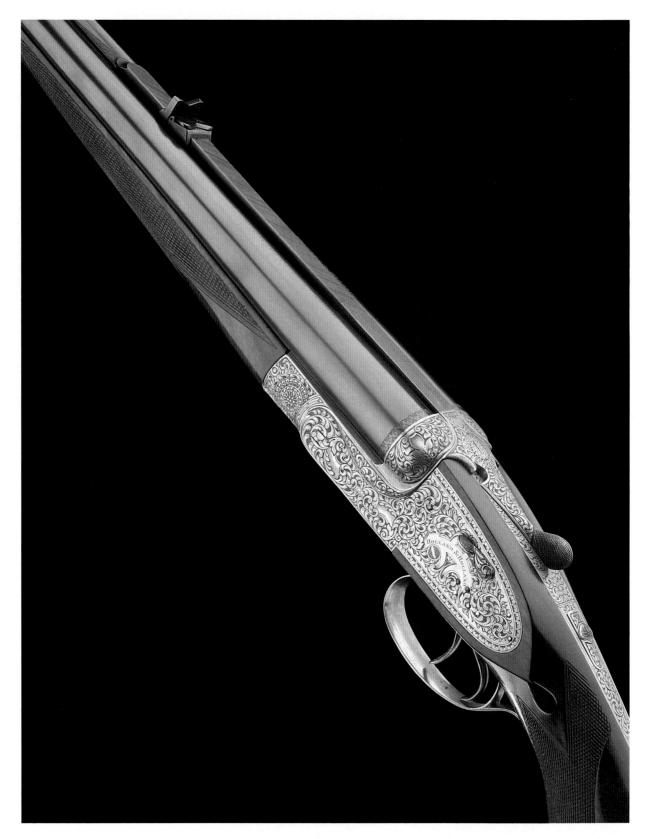

PLATE 18   A .458 (Winchester Magnum) 'Royal' double-barrelled sidelock ejector rifle by Holland & Holland, No. 35484, completed *circa* 1973.

in 1985, with the service pressures marked as kilograms (900 kg) and the chamber length in millimetres (65/70 mm). Whilst there was a brief period (1985-1989) when either Imperial or metric marks could be chosen, this new metric form of marking is now, sadly, the only one available.

It is clear from this that it should be possible to work out the approximate age of a gun from its proof marks, but the situation is frequently complicated by reproof or a succession of reproof marks, some of which can obscure previous marks or make them confusing. But there are certain general guidelines and the collector will be well rewarded if he masters them.

The proof marks for rifles and pistols vary considerably, and because the marks are more erratic they can be very confusing. Since 1855, for example, all rifle barrels should theoretically be stamped with a bore number, but this is quite often not the case, particularly with small bore rifles. There is a greater variation in the form of marking in rifle barrels but there are, nevertheless, certain regular features. Double rifles are generally marked with a bore number indicating the nominal calibre (25 = .577, 52 = .450) and rifles are marked by calibre from about 1887 onwards. As with shotguns, marks introduced in 1887 might include a particular load which will be the equivalent of the 'nitro proof' (for example Rifleite, Cordite), and, from 1925, the nominal case length will be marked (.400 3 in.), as will the specific powder to be used, its weight in grains and the weight of the bullet in grains. Prior to 1904, the marks might include 'BALL'. Pressure markings were introduced in 1954 and the rifle will therefore bear the calibre marking, the nominal case length and the service pressures in tons per square inch. In the period 1925 to 1983 the calibre might sometimes be expressed in metric, but the case length will be in Imperial. In common with shotguns, metric marks were introduced in 1985.

The markings for pistols, unless they are proofed relatively recently, are particularly vague and one is unlikely to find any form of calibre marking between 1855 and 1925. Markings were introduced in 1925 which, as with rifles, included the calibre and nominal case lengths and from 1954 one will find the service pressures expressed as tons per square inch.

The actual proof status of a shotgun will be determined by measuring the internal diameter of the bores, the reading being taken at 9 in. from the breech with a bore micrometer, and then comparing that reading with the bore size marked on the barrels. This bore size (12, 20, 13/1, .740) will not, of course, be the *actual* bore diameter, but each bore size marking is given a maximum size beyond which the gun will be 'out of proof'. Once the *actual* bore diameter reaches that point, the gun will be 'out of proof' and will need therefore to be reproved; proof stages are set at standard intervals (averaging .010 in.), but all that needs to be used to ascertain whether a gun is either in or out of proof is a bore-micrometer and a set of proof tables. It really is as simple as that, though there are occasionally complications; for example, guns proved under the 1868 rules and before the introduction of the subdivision of bore sizes will still theoretically be in proof under the old rules when their bore diameters are oversize by the 1887 Rules – as the 1868 Rules only provided for whole bore-numbers.

The question of the 'proof' status of a gun is most importantly a mark of

A Webley 1902 Patent 12-bore falling-block pendulum proof gun by Webley & Scott, No. 93: 3317. Designed specifically for the task of testing cartridges, the pendulum gun was introduced in answer to the problem of tracing the co-relation of pressure, velocity and recoil when testing cartridges. In considering this problem, the designers had to find a way of translating recoil into an absolute measure, or in other words, to express recoil in units which were equally applicable, whatever the weight of the gun. The method of suspending a gun by four stranded steel wires almost entirely eliminated friction and ensured that each successive swing of the gun on firing was less than the previous one by a very small fraction, thereby ensuring a greater accuracy in the calculations necessary for measuring the momentum on firing.

the legality of the gun and it is normally very unlikely for an enlarged bore diameter to be of any consequence to the safety or material strength of the gun. An enlarged bore might even help to reduce the recoil of a gun as the pressures will not be so tightly confined. Obviously, this situation can be different with those guns that have reached the very end of their *nominal* bore size and which through excessive enlargement of their *actual* bore diameter are about to enter the range of the next nominal bore size up the scale (from '12' to '10', for example). The question of safety in use, however, applies far more to wall thickness measurements and here, because there are no legally established standards, there is the greatest likelihood of confusion. There is no legal minimum thickness for a shotgun barrel, although the British Gun Trade Association *recommend* 20 thousandths of an inch as a general minimum. It is, however, vital for the life-expectancy and safety of the gun that the barrels are of a sufficient thickness. A good overall thickness provides for a lifetime of cleaning, polishing, reblueing and for the removal of flaws such as pits, dents and bulges – and the gun, if the thicknesses are good, may go on to last indefinitely. Some guns, however, are built with relatively thin barrels, and others can become thin as the result of bad workmanship or a combination of the processes mentioned above.

Thin barrels can be a liability in the unlikely event of using a faulty cartridge that might generate excessive pressures on being fired. Under these conditions, the barrel might produce a serious bulge or burst, whereas one with good measurements probably would not. The problem of thin walls is further complicated by flaws such as rivels, packing-bulges, dents, bulges and pits all of which, if severe enough, will require remedial action before their presence affects the shooting and safety of the gun. Under these circumstances, a thin shotgun barrel will require particularly careful repair. Wall thickness measurements are determined on special wall thickness gauges which are not difficult to use but do require a certain amount of basic expertise. A collector who has no intention of using the gun he buys but buys because the gun will fit a space in his collection need not concern himself unduly with the question of wall thicknesses. Knowledge of the wall thickness measurements of a gun is vital though, if the gun is to be used or sold to someone who is likely to want to use it.

It is important to remember that lightweight guns are very often built with lightweight, and therefore relatively thin barrels. English over-and-under guns are also liable to have thin barrels, for the simple reason that as these guns tend to be heavier because of the depth of the actions, greater efforts have to be made to lighten the gun by taking metal from the barrels and hollowing out the stocks. Over-and-under barrels also tend to have 'lop-sided' thicknesses, particularly with the over barrel. This should not be a problem, unless the barrels are very thin, but it requires a very careful measuring of the barrels to ascertain the real thickness readings. Some people use a wall-thickness gauge quickly and haphazardly and, for obvious reasons, will quit when they find an acceptable reading. Using a wall-thickness gauge requires that as much as possible of the surface of the barrels is covered, accurately and carefully, and that if a thin spot is found, that the gauge is re-zeroed and the area checked again. Some gauges have a stabilizing bar which helps to hold the barrel in position when further checking is necessary and which also holds the rods of the gauge firmly in position so that it is not possible to knock or jar the gauge and therefore obtain a false reading.

The requirement for guns to have good wall thickness measurements is very important, but it has become something of a mania in recent years.

A dramatic barrel burst on a boxlock ejector gun. The burst has torn away part of the action and removed the other barrel in its entirety. Any burst is dangerous but, fortunately, the tendency is for the charge and debris to blast away from the firer and the recorded instances of serious injury resulting from accidents of this sort are relatively few.

I have seen a huge number of guns that have had thin barrels – some have even had holes in them – many of which were in use up to the time they were sent in for examination, and whilst I wouldn't recommend barrels like this for use, I would encourage a certain 'leeway' when considering thicknesses.

Remember also that best English guns are largely hand built and that barrel makers would judge the majority of their work by eye and not by machine. Bear in mind also that the wonderful handling qualities of a prized gun are very much a product of these individual skills and are not usually achieved through gauges or machines. If your gun has thin barrels that aren't dangerous, use it carefully.

'Material' alterations to gun barrels can also prove problematical. Perhaps the most serious of these is chamber lengthening which, when carried out without a subsequent proof test, can be dangerous. All guns are chambered and proved for a particular cartridge length and, therefore, for the pressures generated by that particular cartridge. In England, the $2\frac{1}{2}$ in. cartridge has always been the favoured cartridge for a 12-bore game gun. There are, of course, other cartridge lengths for other, more specialised forms of shooting – the 2 in. cartridge for ultra lightweight guns, the $2\frac{3}{4}$ and 3 in. cartridge for pigeon shooting and wild-fowling for example – but the vast majority of English game-guns are chambered $2\frac{1}{2}$ in. Guns built for use on the Continent and in the United States tend to have $2\frac{3}{4}$ in. chambers (for a 12-bore) and this difference in cartridge length is still very much the same today. Problems usually occur when English $2\frac{1}{2}$ in. chambered guns are shipped abroad for use. In the United States, where there are no proof laws, $2\frac{1}{2}$ in. guns are usually re-chambered to $2\frac{3}{4}$ in. and, because of the absence of regulations, they are not reproved for the longer cartridge. It is clear that a gun built and proved to accept pressures at a particular level must not be subjected to higher pressures until it has been tested – unfortunately this is not always done, and it is important to measure the chambers of a gun to make sure that they have not been extended in the past. Any re-chambering requires re-proof.

Other material alterations frequently involve work on the lumps of the barrels. As these are usually the sole means of securing the barrels to the action, any work that requires re-setting loose lumps also requires re-proof. We have already seen how the lumps are secured to the barrels – in the case of chopper lumps, the lumps are already an integral part of the substance of the barrel and this method is therefore the strongest and most reliable. In those methods where the lumps are built as a separate part and then inserted between the barrels or brazed to the underside, it is possible for them to work loose. Dovetail and through lumps are the next strongest method of securing the lumps because these methods also involve mechanical strength and not simply the strength imparted by brazing as is the case with drop and table lumps. Nevertheless, I have encountered almost equal numbers of loose dovetail and drop lumps and the solution is to re-set and reprove.

All guns should be checked for 'looseness' at regular intervals – this looseness is usually not the result of loose lumps but of wear on the hinge-pin or to the bearing surfaces of the lumps and bolt. Work to remedy this does not require a reproof and usually involves renewing the hinge-pin, replacing part of the worn bearing-surface of the lump (usually the front-lump) or working on the bolt and rear lump to effect tightening. Sometimes guns are found to have been 'tightened' by having their action 'squeezed' – this is not a recommended way to tighten the barrels and the action.

Other problems can affect the bores themselves, and these are normally encountered in the form of pitting, dents, bulges and general corrosion. Both the inner and outer surfaces of the barrels should be viewed, with a source of bright unrefracted light so that a line of light is thrown down the barrels towards the eye. The line of light will appear to be broken or thrown out of line where there are dents and bulges. Very often repaired dents and bulges will show up, as will rivels – a series of undulations along the barrel. Pits will appear as dark cavities where the pitting is serious, and small speckles where it is less so. There are many variations in between, the most serious type of pitting being that which occurs on the inner side of the barrel. This is a particularly serious type because it is so difficult to judge how deep it is, and because it lies on the inner side it is not possible to see whether it goes right through the barrel. A very fine-pointed probe will give an idea of the depth of the pit, but buyers of guns should be very wary of guns where there is any indication of deep pitting. Many people fail to see even the most obvious signs of corrosion in shotgun barrels – they tend to look at the light at the end of the barrel rather than directly at the barrel wall. This is not as idiotic as it might at first seem – most people are overawed by the brightness of the shine that is given off even by corroded barrels and assume that because it is bright, it must be clean.

This, of course, is not so – the brightness can hide a variety of unpleasant surprises. It is usually possible to rectify most of the defects found in shotgun barrels but this depends very much on the thickness of the metal – as we have seen, thin barrels with severe pitting are usually best left alone and unused; any attempt to remove the pitting will simply reduce the thicknesses even more. There is another type of pitting which is occasionally found on the outer surfaces of the barrels or action. This is usually a clear sign that the gun has been left in a damp case for a while – and the pitting will be found on the side of the barrels or action which has been in contact with the damp part of the case – usually the spine or base. Dents occur through clumsiness or accidents and if they are severe will give rise to bulges. Bulges occur when the pressures passing up the barrel meet an obstruction and the sudden checking of the pressures cause an instantaneous build-up of pressure which bulges the wall. Sometimes this can cause a 'burst' which is potentially very dangerous indeed. Bursts can be caused by sudden excessive pressures, by obstructions and by material weaknesses in the barrel. We have seen how re-chambering can lead to the use of inappropriately powerful cartridges – sometimes the barrel will bulge or burst as a result, and the same will be true when there is an obstruction in the barrel, such as a plug of mud or snow or a residual piece of the cartridge.

There are, in addition to these inherent problems with barrels, other modifications that can affect the value of a best gun, and these include re-barrelling and barrel shortening. Detection of re-barrelling can be a complex procedure highly dependent upon a clear understanding of the proof marks to be found on the

barrel flats and the action table. For example, an older gun fitted with new barrels in recent times should bear one distinct set of proof marks, but great confusion can be caused by the addition of reproof marks. At all times, great attention should be paid to the name and address on the top rib. If, for example, the address postdates the serial number of the guns, it is quite possible that re-barrelling may have taken place, just as the appearance of a name or address other than that of the maker (which almost always also appears on the action or lockplates) would indicate newer or different barrels. Fortunately some of our greatest gunmakers maintain precise records of their guns, their original specifications, and subsequent alterations – Purdey's, for example, have maintained marvellously accurate records of virtually all their guns and the same also is true of Holland & Holland, Boss, Churchill, Grant, Beesley and others. Nevertheless, a call to one of these makers should confirm or rapidly dispel any doubts over the authenticity of the barrels, as the original length and the chambering are nearly always recorded. As an added complication, rebarrelling by someone other than the maker, which is of considerable detriment to the value of the gun, can sometimes be disguised by faking the original maker's name and address on the barrels.

It is possible also to encounter guns that have spurious proof marks, but fortunately this is not common. It is only through a very thorough understanding of the different styles of proof markings that such things can be detected.

Barrel shortening can, in some instances, be detected by immediate referral to the maker's books. At other times, inserts placed at the muzzles in the space between the ribs and shortened or nonexistent choke cones will indicate shortening, which is usually carried out when a new owner finds that he cannot shoot sufficiently well with the original length of barrel. Re-stocking, unlike re-barrelling by someone other than the original maker, is not a threat to the value of the gun. Very often guns are restocked with wood of a better 'figure' and colour, and as stocks require more idiosyncratic fashioning to suit the buyer, restocking is more commonly practised and more commonly accepted.

There is one more frequently encountered problem associated with barrels that we should deal with before we turn to stocks and actions. Sometimes the ribs that lie between the barrels can loosen and this is detected by suspending the barrels by the lumps from one hand and tapping the barrels with the other. If the ribs are solid the barrels should ring true, rather in the manner of a bell. The sound should be crisp and bright and should not be dull. If loose ribs are tapped hard enough they will 'clank' where they are loose. They should be reset as a matter of urgency because moisture will seep under the rib and set up corrosion in the rib spaces. The barrels of most guns, if they are sound, will ring well, but it is usually the case with Holland & Holland self-opening guns, where the self-opening slide and plunger are fixed to the underside of the barrels towards the breech, that the addition dampens any ring in the barrels. This does not indicate any loosening in the ribs, but is simply the result of the addition of the self-opening mechanism to the barrels.

Gun actions have relatively few problems, but when problems occur, they tend to be quite serious. It is possible for the action of a gun to develop cracks, and these can occur at several points. Cracks usually occur at the 'bridge' of the action where it joins the bar and very often such cracks are associated with unusually deep proof mark stamps and may have occurred as the result of the forceful blow required to impress the mark. Fortunately cracks such as these are not deemed 'material' to the strength of the action, but where they are excessive, that is extending over an eighth of an inch into the bar they should be repaired and the gun reproved. Much more serious cracks are to be found at the 'radius' – the junction between the breech face and the action bar. In vintage hammer guns, this junction is frequently a simple right-angled join, with no form of additional strengthening. As this part of the gun is subject to severe pressures in the firing of the gun, in time it became apparent that a right-angled junction was not sufficiently strong and the semicircular radius was introduced which imparted greater strength. Occasionally cracks can develop along the radius and they can be potentially dangerous. Sometimes the cracks are no more than fractures in the hardened surface of the steel, caused by the straining apart of the breech face and the action bar as the gun is used – these are not, strictly, anything to cause concern. On occasion they are more serious and can extend along the radius and down the sides of the action bar. It is difficult to establish the reason for their occurrence; the 'squeezing' of the action bar as a means of tightening the gun, or a succession of reproofs, sometimes over a long period of time may serve to weaken the action at this point and thereby promote cracks; it might be a matter of the quality of steel (and sometimes iron) used in the manufacture of the action; or the result of using inappropriate cartridges – that is, cartridges generating pressures higher than the pressures the gun was designed for. Whatever the cause, a high magnification glass should be used to examine the radius of any sporting shotgun. If a hairline crack is detected, specialist engineering advice should be sought and the gun submitted to one of the Proof Houses for an opinion.

It is possible to weld such flaws, but it is always best to avoid guns with this sort of problem. It is now relatively common to find lightweight boxlock guns with cracked actions, and those guns where very little of the metal of the action is taken away tend to be more resilient. Backlock guns and back-action sidelocks tend to be stronger for this reason.

The problems encountered with stocks tend to be more normally associated with the 'fit' of the gun. Guns are to be found with shortened or extended stocks, with leather-covered cheekpads and with extreme variations in cast. In general, it is better for a gun to have a stock that is longer than average because it can always be shortened. Very short stocks will need to be replaced or extended but it is very difficult to get different pieces of wood to match and extensions are usually rather unsightly. Perhaps the best compromise is to add a leather-covered recoil pad to to the butt, which will preserve the appearance of a gun, more than wooden extensions.

Certain gunmakers fashion stocks in differing ways. Many Churchill guns, for example, will have relatively short stocks, a dogleg cast and an offset comb; the only possible reason for this is that many Churchill guns were built for short stout men with heavily-jowelled

An action failure on a Grant sidelever gun. The illustration shows how the fracture has occurred just short of the radial junction between the breech face and the action bar and at a critical structural point.

The 'fluted' fences and the close foliate-cross engraving are typical Grant decorative motifs.

This barrel burst is further away from the action body but it has occurred much closer to the firer's hand.

faces! Rather like Mr Churchill himself. The same observation also explains Mr Churchill's fondness for 25 in. barrelled guns, which might have been introduced to make portly gentlemen quicker onto their quarry. Many Holland guns also have 'swept' combs which probably accommodate the face well.

Cracks will also develop in stocks, and will usually be easier to find than cracks in the action. The stock should be examined carefully with a particular concentration on the 'hand' – the part of the stock which joins the 'body' of the stock to the 'head' where it joins the action. The hand is the thinnest and therefore the most vulnerable part of the stock. A line should be followed along both sides of the bottom strap, around the under-and-over horns (in sidelocks) and down the top strap. Cracks occur in this area because of the flexing that occurs when the gun is fired and also because it is the part most closely in contact with the action and furniture, where oil from these parts is most likely to invade and soften the wood. Sometimes these cracks lead into the chequering and may seem to disappear – a magnifying glass will soon help to trace any continuation along the groove of a chequering cut. It is possible to repair cracks in stocks, but this, of course, is very much dependent upon the severity of the crack. Methods of repair include drying the oil out of the stock, glueing and plugging, but sometimes the stock will need to be replaced. In sidelocks unseen cracks can occur at the 'head' of the stock beneath the lockplates. Quite often they will remain unnoticed, secured as they are by the support of the lockplates, but bad cracks will often be detected by a tremor in the 'hand' of the stock when the gun is opened and closed. The usual remedy for cracks of this sort is to glue and plug and then, perhaps, to screw in a supporting plate. In boxlocks, the same problem, or at least, a similar one, occurs when the wood springs at the head; this is usually remedied by plugging the wood at this point.

Extreme variations in cast will sometimes be encountered, the usual reason being that they are a method of allowing a right-handed shot to accommodate a left master eye and vice versa. Boxlock guns that are cast off or on towards central vision or across-eyed will be easier to restock than sidelocks because it is normally only the furniture that is bent. Sidelock guns with extreme cast of one or other type will also normally have not only bent furniture, but bent lockplates as well. Restocking is a straightforward gunmaking procedure, but bending back lockplates and lockwork is a very involved process indeed and it is normally best to try to find someone who needs that type of cast rather than to convert the gun back to a more normal appearance.

There are a myriad of other problems associated with guns of all types. These can include faulty ejector work which can lead to a complete lack of ejection of the spent case or to erratic 'timing'; blunt or misshapen strikers which can result in a lack of detonation; poor extractor fit resulting in delayed or imperfect ejection; worn lockwork and poor trigger pulls. Other problems, as we have seen, will affect self-opening and single trigger mechanisms – the addition of one or more complicated mechanisms can always lead to problems. In general, single triggers can wear out or lose their function when the wood swells around the mechanism in a poorly seasoned or badly fitting stock, but the problems affecting self-opening mechanisms tend to be mild by comparison and the results

Boss 12-bore sidelock
ejector gun No. 5858 built
circa 1910. The stock is
completely cracked
through the hand – the
point at which virtually all
fractures occur.

much less frustrating – a self-opening mechanism does not, after all, affect the actual firing sequence of a gun.

There is nothing, however, that cannot be done to repair a sporting gun. Worn out barrels can be repaired, cracked stocks can be renewed and flaws in actions can be repaired. Smaller jobs such as the renewal of broken lock and ejector work are very much part of the routine maintenance of a gun and the only real deterrent to the amount of work required is cost. At today's prices, for example, rebarrelling for a best gun can cost anything up to about £8000, and restocking up to or about half that amount. Ultimately, and assuming that the money required is to hand, the major consideration, particularly with a best gun, should be to maintain not only the function of the gun, but also its value. A good Purdey should not, therefore, be sleeved; it should be sent to the makers for new barrels. In every instance where restocking is required, a best gun should be given highly-figured wood and any other work should be carried out competently and carefully by a qualified gunsmith. The British trade is fortunate today in having a good number of highly skilled gunsmiths who have trained with one or other of our great gunmakers and there is no excuse for ending up with poor or faulty repair work.

8

The Market

As in most other collectable fields, the emphasis is very much upon the best makers. The market for sporting guns and rifles however, is unusual in one particular and very important respect – most of the guns will be bought to be used and the most desirable characteristics therefore become a combination of what are, traditionally the best names and what are, in practice, the most efficient and effective handling characteristics. As regards the latter, the toplever, for example, has become the most preferred method of opening a gun and even though there are some very good examples of Grant and Boss sidelever guns to be had they start with an immediate disadvantage. Secondly, very few shooting men want to shoot all day with a heavy gun, unless of course the quarry is duck or wildfowl. This explains the growing fondness for light 12-bore guns shooting light loads such as the 1 oz and the $1\frac{1}{16}$ oz. It also explains, to a certain extent, the gradual shift away from 12-bore guns to 20-bores and, where the cost of these is too high, to 16-bores.

This is particularly the case with older men who find a 12-bore rather tiring. There is, similarly, a dislike of short or overly long barrels and whilst 25 in. barrels are perhaps ideal for grouse or partridge (and they will certainly have their devoted followers for all other forms of shooting) and for people of shorter stature, the classic length barrel remains 28 in., with 30 in. or 27 in. following close behind.

There is also the habit of tradition which will act as a market force. There is still, for example, considerable dislike of the over-and-under configuration in a game gun amongst certain shooting men. Burrard was quite vociferous in his dislike of these guns and the same attitude is quite commonly encountered today – despite the fact that the best English over-and-under guns are the most beautifully built and that they are capable of holding their own in both looks and usage alongside side-by-sides. The same tradition acts very firmly when one is considering the decoration of a gun.

Foliate-scroll engraving has, for centuries, been one of the most common and widely accepted decorative motifs and the market today is quite clearly divided between those who like 'rose and scroll' engraving, and those who prefer game scenes. It is very rare to find someone who can appreciate both forms dispassionately and I think there can be little doubt that the overall weight of favour lies with the traditional forms.

There are two final points concerning the 'marketability' of guns. It is sometimes a practise to re colour-harden a gun to improve its appearance. This can sometimes be detected by the presence of worn engraving under the finish and it remains a negative factor in the saleability of most guns. It can be of lesser

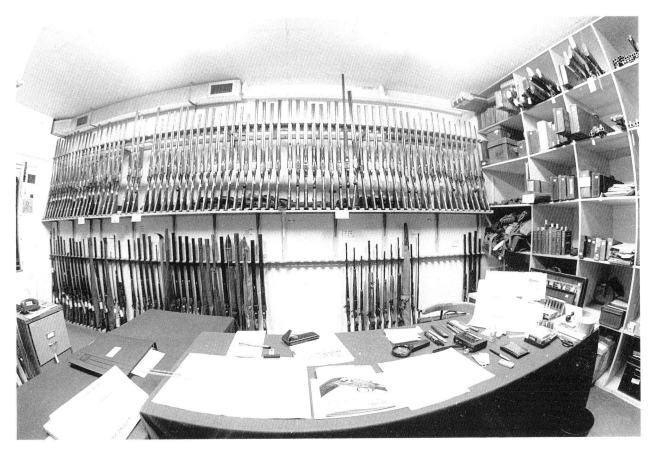

The Gun Room.

importance with second or third quality guns but it should be viewed with considerable suspicion when applied to best guns particularly when it has been done to make them appear to be unused.

Another negative factor is sleeving, in which old and unsafe barrels have new tubes sleeved onto the existing breech-ends. Whilst sleeving provides a new set of barrels at a fraction of the cost of true rebarrelling it should only be done to best guns *in extremis*. A better solution, in the absence of the requisite funds, would be to keep the original barrels to maintain the authenticity of the gun and to have new less expensive barrels made elsewhere.

But what of the makers? Each of our leading makers have their devoted followers; the following are a few brief, personal observations:

Purdey's (founded 1814): I have seen and examined more guns by this maker than any other and there can be no doubt that they have built guns of superlative quality for a very, very long time. For a gunmaking concern of their size, Purdey's have produced a remarkably large number of guns, most of which, it can be argued, are still in use today. Their number at auction is far greater than any other maker. Some people do not like the Purdey self-opening system, finding it rather too fierce, but this is not significant.

Holland & Holland (founded 1835): a maker justly famous for producing, with only one or two exceptions, the best double rifles in the world. Their production can be confusing as they have, unlike Boss and Purdey's, produced a considerable number of different grades of gun. The ultimate Holland & Holland shotgun remains the 'Royal Brevis Self-Opener' (introduced in 1922) but they also produce 'Modele de Luxe' guns with extra finish. In practice, the preference for Holland & Holland or Purdey's, lies with the *appearance* of the guns; Holland's have a generally bolder style of engraving which some people prefer.

Boss (founded 1812): Boss are, perhaps, the most idiosyncratic of makers and they remain famous for two particular things:(i) their over-and-under design and (ii) their single-trigger mechanism, both of which are masterpieces of design. Boss are also the makers of what is perhaps the world's rarest gun – the Boss over-and-under double rifle, but I understand that they are now planning a new production of these guns. Unlike the design of a Purdey which has remained essentially unchanged from the 1880s, Boss guns will be encountered with a comparatively large number of cosmetic differences. The earlier guns, for example, built in the 1890s, were not stocked to the fences as are all Purdey's, and many have a large 'BOSS'S PATENT' marking on the sides of the action body that is not generally liked. The overall style of the engraving is also often quite different, not only in appearance, but also in the means of execution, and this is so even between guns built within a few years of each other. In recent years, the most desirable Boss gun, in addition to the over-and-under, has become the 'round body self-opener' fitted with a single trigger (8000 series guns).

Woodward (founded 1827): it is still not generally accepted that there are, in fact, a 'top four' rather than a 'top three' and Woodward guns form the addition. The most desirable Woodward remains the over-and-under design which was subsequently adopted by Purdey's following their purchase of the Woodward name in 1948. Woodward guns tend to be heavier in appearance than any of the other 'best' makers and their sidelocks are characterized by arcaded fences, protruding tumbler pivots and the early trade name 'Automatic'. They are all beautifully made.

But what of the other makers? By these I mean makers such as Atkin, Beesley, Churchill, Dickson, Gibbs, Grant, Greener, Lancaster, Lang, Rigby, Westley Richards, Watson, Wilkes, and also Bland, Evans, Harrison & Hussey, Hellis and Jeffery. Some of these are still going, many along traditional lines as independent London or Birmingham-based concerns, but others have amalgamated or disappeared altogether. The histories of Churchill's, Atkin, Grant and Lang, for example, have become intermingled over the years despite the fact that they all started life separately.

Churchill's started in 1891 as E.J. Churchill, based in Agar Street, London WC2; Henry Atkin Ltd was formed in 1904 and was initially based in Jermyn Street; Stephen Grant started in 1866 in St James's Street and Joseph Lang & Son were established in 1875 on the foundations of a much older company. All remained more or less independent until 1960, with the exception of minor amalgamations such as those of Grant and Lang in 1925, Harrison & Hussey with Grant & Lang in 1930 and subsequent additions to this nucleus such as those of Charles Lancaster in 1932 and Frederick Beesley in 1939. In 1960 all these companies joined together, presumably as both the demand for various types of gun and the market in general contracted.

Most English makers are famous for one or other thing: Churchill's for their 'Premiere' grade guns and for the introduction of 25 in. barrels; Rigby's for their double rifles, Mauser stalking rifles and dipped edge lockplate shotguns; Grant's for their best lightweight guns and the use of sidelevers; Atkins for their 'Spring-Opener' self-opening system which is similar to the original Purdey or Beesley action but with different ejector work; and so on. The list is very long indeed and it testifies to one very important point. All these makers could, quite easily, be classified as 'best' makers for they all produced guns that are every bit as good as a Boss or Purdey; there won't be anything in a comparison of best Boss or Grant or Churchill actions built in the twenties and thirties – with slight differences in design, they will all be beautifully built. The central, pivotal point to remember about classic 'best' English guns no matter who the maker is that they were all the product of generations of devoted and ingenious craftsmen.

And what of the marketplace? London continues to be the focus of best gunmaking. With the exception of Brescia in Northern Italy where there is a great concentration of makers, including fashionable makers such as Fabbri, Famars and Rizzini, and Birmingham and Edinburgh who feature Westley Richards and Dickson's respectively, the weight of tradition lies firmly with London. Here are to be found the remaining 'best' makers, together with a number of other businesses supplying ancillary goods such as sporting accessories; here also are the auction houses specialising in the sale of sporting guns, and some dealers.

There is a tradition of 'outworking' in the English gun trade and this is particularly prevalent today. Most of the gunmakers who have chosen a more independent life have worked for one or other of the great makers and it is now possible to have a gun made from barrels, stocks, and actions built in several different locations. There is also a nationwide network of gun dealers, specialising in best English guns.

9

Auction Price Guide

The following price guide is based upon a three year span (1991–1993/4) of auction prices at Christie's which are, in general, somewhat lower than those to be found in the full retail section of the market. It should be pointed out that, whilst any good auction house will provide a comprehensive guide to the condition of the guns they are selling, including complete lists of bore dimension and wall thickness measurements, buying at auction is very much *caveat emptor*. A dealer, on the other hand, will normally supply a full money back guarantee after a specific interval and will also normally supply free repair work within a certain date of the purchase of the gun.

The reason for higher retail prices (although there have been many exceptions to this at auction) is simply that a dealer will almost certainly have to undertake some repair or renovation work prior to a sale and he must also consider other factors such as overheads and profits. All the major auction houses charge a commission to the seller and a premium to the buyer and the price guides set out below are based upon prices which are inclusive of the premium paid.

I have devised three categories for the better-known English makers which will, in general, cover the condition of most guns. These are:

a) good to excellent
b) average to good
c) defective/poor to average.

All three are to be applied to the majority of the following:

1   Pairs of sidelock ejector guns
2   Single sidelock ejector guns
3   Pairs of boxlock ejector guns
4   Single boxlock ejector guns
5   Round action ejector guns
6   Over-and-under guns
7   Back action guns
8   Non-ejector guns
9   Hammer and hammer ejector guns and rifles
10 Sporting rifles
11 Accessories
12 Unusual guns

Pairs of best sporting guns remain very much in demand and the following three classes give a good, representative selection of types and condition. For obvious reasons, category (a) includes those guns retaining a good deal of their original finish. They also have classic specifications in terms of weight, and barrel and stock lengths. Those in categories (b) and (c) will have lesser amounts of finish and sometimes none at all. Those guns encountered of category (c) type will have considerable wear to the stocks, actions and barrels and sometimes to all three. There will, in some instances, be particular problems with wall thickness and bore diameter measurements; the minimum price now for a pair of best guns in poor condition and without their barrels appears to be about £6,000 (1994).

It is desirable for pairs of guns to have been built at the same time and to have consecutive serial numbers. Those guns built as 'matched' or 'composed' pairs will have a disadvantage but this can be overcome when they possess excellent characteristics in terms of finish or specification. A good pair of guns is worth somewhat more than two good singles. Factors such as long stock extensions, poor wood, cracked stocks and Damascus barrels will affect the prices downwards.

Occasionally trios of best guns will be encountered. These are usually in fairly good to worn condition and they are always of interest. Values at current levels vary between approximately £15,000 to £25,000 for good examples but it is rare to find any in excellent condition. Trios are also commonly encountered as a pair with one other associated gun. True trios, built with consecutive numbers will command a premium.

1   *Pairs of sidelock ejector guns*

a) **Good to excellent condition: £20,000 – £30,000 +**

J. PURDEY: a pair of 12-bore ($2\frac{3}{4}$ in.) self-opening sidelock ejector guns No. 28851/2 (1986); rolled-edge triggerguards, best bouquet and scroll engraving with full hardening colour and blueing, well-figured stocks, chopper lump barrels with matt game ribs; weight 6 lb 13 oz (No. 1) and 6 lb 12 oz (No. 2), $14\frac{3}{4}$ in. stocks, 28 in. barrels, choke approx. $\frac{1}{4}$ & $\frac{1}{2}$ (No. 1) and I.C. & $\frac{1}{2}$ (No. 2), $2\frac{3}{4}$ in. chambers, nitro proof; cased.

BOSS: a pair of lightweight 12-bore round body single trigger self-opening sidelock ejector guns No. 8599/600 (1938); Boss patent single triggers with rolled-edge triggerguards, best bouquet and scroll engraving with some hardening colour, well-figured stocks with semi-pistolgrips and leather-covered recoil pads, chopper lump barrels with game ribs; weight 6 lb 4 oz, $14\frac{3}{8}$ in. pulls, 27 in. barrels, approx. I.C. & $\frac{1}{4}$ choke, $2\frac{1}{2}$ in. chambers, nitro proof; cased.

HOLLAND & HOLLAND: a pair of 12-bore ($2\frac{3}{4}$ in.) 'Royal Self-Opener' sidelock ejector guns No. 36910/11 (1970); hand-detachable locks, rolled-edge triggerguards, best engraving of bold foliate scrolls with full hardening colour and blueing, well-figured stocks, chopper lump barrels with game ribs; weight 6 lb 10 oz, $15\frac{3}{4}$ in. stocks, 28 in. barrels, choke approx. I.C. & $\frac{1}{2}$ (No. 1) and $\frac{3}{8}$ & $\frac{1}{2}$ (No. 2), $2\frac{3}{4}$ in. chambers, nitro proof; cased.

b) Average to good condition: £10,000 – £20,000

F. BEESLEY: a pair of 12-bore single trigger sidelock ejector guns No. 1745/6 (1903); non-selective single triggers, the fences chiselled in relief with acanthus foliage, best bouquet and scroll engraving with traces of hardening colour, well-figured stocks with leather-covered recoil pads, Whitworth steel chopper lump barrels with game-ribs and scroll-engraved breech ends; weight 6 lb 12 oz, $15\frac{1}{8}$ in. pulls, $29\frac{3}{4}$ in. barrels, all approx. cyl., $2\frac{1}{2}$ in. chambers, nitro reproof (1992); cased.

C. LANCASTER: a pair of lightweight 12-bore 'Twelve Twenty' assisted-opening sidelock ejector guns No. 17119/20 (1935); Baker patent assisted-opening action, fluted fences, the undersides of the action bars inlaid in gold with 'The Twelve Twenty', best bouquet and scroll engraving with traces of hardening colour, well-figured stocks, chopper lump barrels with game ribs; weight 5 lb 15 oz, $14\frac{1}{4}$ in. stocks, 28 in. barrels, approx. $\frac{1}{4}$ & $\frac{5}{8}$ choke, $2\frac{1}{2}$ in. chambers, nitro proof (No. 2 left barrel thickness marginal); cased.

E.J. CHURCHILL: a pair of lightweight 12-bore 'Premiere XXV' assisted-opening sidelock ejector guns, No. 5351/2 (1936); Baker patent assisted-opening action, double rolled-edge triggerguards, best close foliate-scroll engraving with traces of hardening colour, highly-figured stocks, chopper lump barrels with Churchill ribs and scroll-engraved breech ends; weight 5 lb $15\frac{1}{2}$ oz, $14\frac{7}{8}$ in. stocks, 25 in. barrels, all approx. $\frac{1}{2}$ choke, $2\frac{1}{2}$ in. chambers, nitro proof; cased.

c) Defective/poor to average condition: Best £5,000 – £10,000, others £3,000 – £8,000

J. PURDEY: a pair of 12-bore self-opening sidelock ejector guns No. 23445/6 (1928); *without barrels*; rounded bars, best bouquet and scroll engraving, brushed bright finish, well-figured stocks with leather-covered recoil pads; $14\frac{7}{8}$ in. pulls; cased.

BOSS: a pair of lightweight 12-bore round body single trigger self-opening sidelock ejector guns No. 8317/8 (1935); No. 2 *without barrels*; full self-opening action, Boss patent single triggers with rolled-edge triggerguards, best bouquet and scroll engraving, figured replacement stock with recoil pad (No. 1), well-figured stock with recoil pad (No. 2), the chopper lump barrels with game rib (No. 1 only); $15\frac{1}{4}$ in. pulls: No. 1 only, weight 6 lb 3 oz, 27 in. barrels, approx. cyl. and $\frac{3}{8}$ choke, $2\frac{1}{2}$ in. chambers, nitro reproof; cased.

H. ATKIN: a pair of 12-bore ($2\frac{3}{4}$ in.) 'Spring-Opener' sidelock ejector guns No. 2971/2 (1930); full self-opening action, best bouquet and scroll engraving with traces of hardening colour, boldly-figured stocks with extensions (No. 1 cracked and repaired at the head), rebarrelled (chopper lump) by H. Atkin, with game ribs; weight 6 lb 10 oz, 15 in. pulls, 28 in. barrels, approx. $\frac{1}{4}$ & $\frac{1}{2}$ choke, $2\frac{3}{4}$ in. chambers, nitro proof; cased.

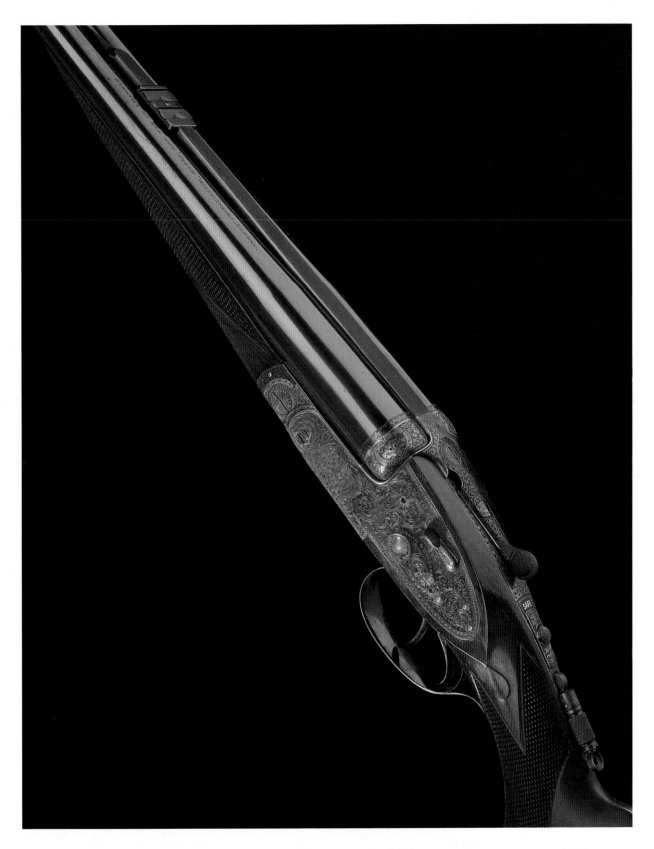

PLATE 19   A fine .375 Magnum (Flanged) 'Royal' double-barrelled sidelock ejector rifle, No. 28428, completed *circa* 1913.

PLATE 20 (*above*) A .458 (Winchester Magnum) double-barrelled 'Royal' sidelock ejector rifle by Holland & Holland, No. 35523; the rifle was commenced *circa* 1979 and completed in 1982. Of note are the bolstered action body, the hand detachable locks and the Monte Carlo comb with cheek piece. (*right*) A .400/.360 ($2\frac{3}{4}$ in.) double-barrelled boxlock non-ejector rifle by W. Evans, No. 13895, completed *circa* 1926.

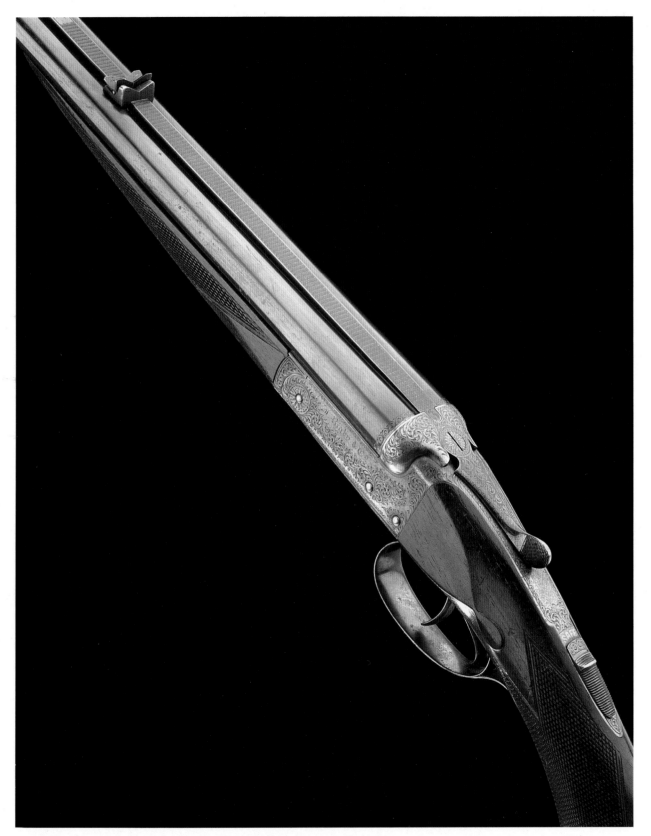

PLATE 21   A .250 double-barrelled boxlock ejector rifle by J. Rigby, No. 17855, completed *circa* 1914. Double rifles built in rook rifle calibres are rare and especially so when built with ejectors.

PLATE 22   Two good examples of increasingly rare pistols. *(above)* A .577 double-barrelled hammer Howdah pistol by Army & Navy. *(below)* A .410 double-barrelled sidelock ejector pistol by L. Douard (Tours), No. 1580. The quality of this most unusual piece is exceptional. The combination of full sidelocks, an ejector system, chopper-lump barrels and the quality and nature of the engraving would indicate that it was intended primarily for display. The engraver, H. Leukers, was acknowledged a Belgian master engraver and was responsible for presenting 23 engraving designs at the Paris Exhibition of 1937; it is almost certainly the case that this pistol comprised part of those designs.

The comments made in the previous section have the same relevance here. Good single guns have become more popular as the demand for driven shooting has declined and there is a particular preference for single guns built as single guns and not, therefore, marked '1' or '2'. Lightweight game guns have become particularly popular; heavy pigeon guns are rarely found as pairs but good single guns will be encountered with extra sets of barrels for true 'live pigeon' shooting as practised, for example, in Monte Carlo in the early decades of this century. The Dickson sidelock in category (b) is included because such guns are not commonly encountered; it is more usual to find Dickson round-action guns *disguised* as sidelocks with dummy sideplates.

2 Single sidelock ejector guns

(a) Good to excellent condition: £8,000 – £15,000 +

HOLLAND & HOLLAND: a 12-bore 'Royal Self-Opener' sidelock ejector gun No. 30776 (1928); hand-detachable locks, rolled-edge triggerguard, best engraving of bold foliate scrolls with much hardening colour and blueing, well-figured stock, the chopper lump barrels with sunken game rib; weight 6 lb 6½ oz, 14¾ in. stock, 30in. barrels, approx. I.C. & ⅜ choke, 2½ in. chambers, nitro proof; cased.

J. PURDEY: a 12-bore (2½ in./2¾ in.) self-opening sidelock ejector gun No. 25440 (1937); best bouquet and scroll engraving with much hardening colour, boldly-figured stock with leather-covered recoil pad, chopper lump barrels with sunken game rib; weight 6 lb 8 oz, 14¾ in. pull, 28 in. barrels, approx. I.C. & ⅜ choke, 2½ in. chambers, nitro proof; with a set of interchangeable extra chopper lump barrels by J. Wilson (1987), with Churchill-style rib; cased.

A Westley Richards three-barrelled single-trigger sidelock ejector gun. Note the 'pyramid' form of construction of the barrels and compare with the Dickson 'in line' arrangement which can be seen on Plate 16.

(b) Average to good condition: £4,000 – £8,000

J. DICKSON: a 12-bore sidelock ejector gun No. 7542 (1957); best bouquet and scroll engraving with some hardening colour, well-figured stock, cast-on for the left shoulder, chopper lump barrels with game rib; weight 6 lb 9 oz, $14\frac{5}{8}$ in. stock, 28 in. barrels, approx. I.C. & $\frac{1}{2}$ choke, $2\frac{1}{2}$ in. chambers, nitro proof.

(c) Defective/poor to average condition: £2,000 – £4,000

HUSSEY & HUSSEY: a 12-bore sidelock ejector gun No. 14565; full game engraving, the lockplates engraved with scenes of pointer and retriever within naturalistic settings, the underside of the action bar similarly engraved, well-figured (?replacement) stock, chopper lump barrels with sunken game-rib; weight 6 lb 10 oz, 15 in. stock, 28 in. barrels, approx. I.C. & $\frac{1}{2}$ choke, $2\frac{1}{2}$ in. chambers, nitro reproof (right barrel thickness below recommended minimum).

3 Pairs of boxlock ejector guns

True *pairs* of boxlock ejector guns are not common. As we have seen, this is very much a cheaper type of gun and pairs of guns for the more expensive forms of shooting were normally ordered as sidelocks. However, a comparison of the costs of pairs of sidelocks and boxlocks will show how much value for money the latter category provides. I have been able to find only one example of a good pair of boxlocks in adequate condition and these happen to be 16-bores; a pair of 12-bore guns with the same amount of finish would be worth the same. Those guns in the higher categories, and this will include single guns, will need to have a number of added embellishments; the Greener in Section 4 is a particularly good example. Occasionally buyers are prepared to pay more for a good, plain gun in excellent condition simply because it will offer excellent value for money when compared with a sidelock in the same condition.

(a) Good to excellent condition: £3,000 – £6,000

GALLYON: a pair of 16-bore ($2\frac{1}{2}$ in./$2\frac{3}{4}$ in.) boxlock ejector guns No. 12041/12088 (1959/1961); scroll-back action bodies, full bouquet and scroll engraving with some hardening colour, the triggerguards engraved with a 'horn of plenty' motif, figured stocks with pistolgrips; weight 5 lb 15 oz (No. 1) and 6 lb 2 oz (No. 2), $14\frac{1}{8}$ in. stocks, 28 in. barrels, choke approx. cyl. & $\frac{1}{2}$ (No. 1) and $\frac{1}{4}$ & $\frac{5}{8}$ (No. 2), $2\frac{1}{2}$ in. chambers (No. 1) and $2\frac{3}{4}$ in. chambers (No. 2), nitro proof; cased.

(b) Average to good condition: £1,500 – £3,000

W. POWELL: a pair of 12-bore single-trigger boxlock ejector guns No. 10406/7; Boss patent single triggers with rolled-edge triggerguards, side-mounted safes, best bouquet and scroll engraving, boldly figured stocks with extensions, No. 1 a replacement, rebrowned Damascus barrels; weight 6 lb 8 oz, $13\frac{3}{4}$ in. pulls, 30 in. barrels, choke approx. $\frac{1}{4}$ & $\frac{3}{8}$ (No. 1) and cyl. & I.C. (No. 2), $2\frac{1}{2}$ in. chambers, nitro reproof; cased.

(c) Defective/poor to average condition: £500 – £1,500

WESTLEY RICHARDS: a matched pair of 12-bore boxlock ejector guns No. B9127/B9149; *without barrels*; bold foliate-scroll engraving, well-figured stocks, gun No. 1 with extension and butt plate, gun No. 2 with butt plate; 15 in. pulls; cased.

(a) **Good to Excellent condition: £2,500 – £4,500**

4 Single boxlock ejector guns

W.W. GREENER: a 12-bore 'Grade G60 Royal' Facile Princeps boxlock ejector gun No. 53146; treble-grip action with manual side safe, arcaded fences, the toplever gold inlaid with a crown, scroll-back action body, best engraving of foliate scrolls with oak leaf borders and game vignettes, boldly-figured stock with decorative horn inserts, Whitworth steel barrels with game rib and scroll-engraved breech ends; weight 6 lb 10 oz, $15\frac{1}{8}$ in. stock, 30 in. barrels, approx. $\frac{1}{2}$ & full choke, $2\frac{1}{2}$ in. chambers, nitro proof.

(b) **Average to good condition: £1,000 – £1,500**

W.R. PAPE: a 12-bore boxlock ejector gun No. 12442, manual safe, the fences engraved with flowers and bold foliate scrolls on a matt ground, full foliate-scroll engraving, well-figured stock with extension; weight 6 lb 6 oz, $14\frac{7}{8}$ in. pull, 30 in. barrels, approx. cyl. & $\frac{3}{4}$ choke, $2\frac{1}{2}$ in. chambers, nitro reproof; cased.

(c) Defective/poor to average condition: £300 – £1,000

W. EVANS: a 12-bore ($2\frac{3}{4}$ in.) boxlock ejector gun No. 5153; the fences chiselled in relief with stylized acanthus foliage, best bouquet and scroll engraving, brushed bright and reblued finish, figured stock; weight 6 lb 7 oz, 15 in. stock, 30 in. barrels, approx. I.C. & $\frac{5}{8}$ choke, $2\frac{3}{4}$ in. chambers, nitro reproof (right barrel-thickness marginal); cased.

The most desirable round action guns are those by Dickson; the earlier guns by MacNaughton have only recently begun to achieve respectable prices, probably because they are perceived to be rather old-fashioned in appearance. The market for Dickson guns has developed over the last five years from the early 1980s, when they were the object of a small number of devotees, to the present day, at which point they have achieved considerable popularity. Their prices, however, still fall somewhat behind those of sidelock guns in comparable condition. Pairs of round action guns are not common and their values range from £6,000 to £10,000 in average condition to as much as £20,000 for those retaining all their original finish.

5 Round action ejector guns

(a) **Good to excellent condition: £8,000 – £10,000**

J. DICKSON: a 12-bore round action ejector gun No. 6979 (1924); best bouquet

An Evans boxlock ejector gun, No. 2721, with characteristic ribanded fences.

and scroll engraving with some hardening colour, finely figured stock, chopper lump barrels with game rib; weight 6 lb 8½ oz, 15½ in. stock, 29 in. barrels, approx. I.C. & ⅝ choke, 2½ in. chambers, nitro proof; cased.

(b) Average to good condition: £4,000 – £8,000

J. DICKSON: a 12-bore round action ejector gun No. 7286 (1934); gold-washed mechanism, best bouquet and scroll engraving, boldly-figured stock with extension, rebarrelled by J. Dickson (1991), with chopper lumps and game rib; weight 6 lb 5 oz, 14⅝ in. pull, 28 in. barrels, approx. ¼ & ¾ choke, 2½ in. chambers, nitro proof; cased.

(c) Defective/poor to average condition: £2,000 – £4,000

J. MACNAUGHTON: a 12-bore round action ejector gun No. 2127; swivel-safe, the top strap inset with a detachable inspection panel, best foliate-scroll engraving, well-figured stock (short crack at the hand) with extension, steel barrels with game rib (loose); weight 6 lb 13½ oz, 15½ in. pull, 28 in. barrels, approx. cyl. & ⅞ choke, 2½ in. chambers, nitro reproof; cased.

6 Over-and-under guns

Pairs of best English over-and-under guns are particularly sought after as are those in smaller bore sizes. In recent years, over-and-under guns have become the vehicle for all manner of decorative embellishments, hence the example of the Purdey engraved by Ken Hunt in category (a). The market can be divided firmly between Boss and Woodward, but Purdey's and Holland & Holland have produced new over-and-under designs in recent years, both of which are extremely elegant. The Woodward in category (c) had some considerable wear to the action but it was, nevertheless, in useable condition.

(a) Good to excellent condition: Pairs £40,000 – £60,000, Single £20,000 – £30,000

BOSS: a pair of light 12-bore over-and-under single-trigger sidelock ejector guns No. 8739/40 (1946); Boss patent single triggers with rolled-edge triggerguards, hold-open toplevers, best bouquet and scroll engraving with much hardening colour, figured stocks, the barrels with breech flats; weight 6 lb 5½ oz, 15⅜ in. stocks, 26 in. barrels, choke approx. I.C. & ¼ (No. 1) and ¼ & ⅜ (No. 2), 2½ in. chambers, nitro proof; cased.

J. PURDEY: a Hunt-engraved 12-bore (3 in. Magnum) single trigger under-and-over sidelock ejector gun No. 28805 (1987); manual safe, hold-open toplever, Purdey non-selective single trigger, the lockplates, action bar and furniture profusely engraved with game scenes, the makers' name inlaid in gold on the lockplates, each lockplate signed 'K.C. Hunt 87', bright finish overall, highly-figured stock with pistolgrip, the barrels with matt ventilated top rib; weight 7 lb 7½ oz, 14¾ in. stock, 27 in. barrels, approx. ⅜ & ⅞ choke, 3 in. magnum chambers, nitro proof (for maximum service pressures of 4 tons); cased.

(b) Average to good condition: Pairs £15,000 – £30,000, Single £10,000 – £20,000

J. WOODWARD: a light 12-bore under-and-over sidelock ejector gun No. 6640 (1922); hold-open toplever, best bouquet and scroll engraving with traces of hardening colour, well-figured stock with butt plate, the barrels with matt top rib; weight 6 lb 3 oz, $14\frac{1}{2}$ in. pull, 28 in. barrels, both approx. $\frac{3}{8}$ choke, $2\frac{1}{2}$ in. chambers, nitro reproof; cased.

J. PURDEY: a 12-bore under-and-over sidelock ejector gun No. 26262 (1951); hold-open toplever, best bouquet and scroll engraving with some hardening colour, figured stock with extension, sling swivels, the barrels with solid top rib; weight 6 lb $14\frac{1}{2}$ oz, $15\frac{1}{8}$ in. pull, 28 in. barrels, approx. I.C. & $\frac{5}{8}$ choke, $2\frac{1}{2}$ in. chambers, nitro proof; with interchangeable extra 'cylinder' barrels with solid top rib; cased.

(c) Defective/poor to average condition: Pairs £10,000 – £15,000, Single guns £5,000 – £10,000

HOLLAND & HOLLAND: a rare 12-bore 'Royal' single trigger assisted open-ing over-and-under backlock ejector gun No. 29092 (1936); *without barrels*; Holland & Holland single trigger with rolled-edge triggerguard, the bolstered action body with hand-detachable locks, best bouquet and scroll engraving, well-figured stock with extension; $14\frac{1}{8}$ in. pull.

J. WOODWARD: a 16-bore ($2\frac{3}{4}$ in.) under-and-over sidelock ejector gun No. 6642 (1922); hold-open toplever, best bouquet and scroll engraving, figured replacement stock with recoil pad, Whitworth steel barrels with matt solid top rib; weight 6 lb 10 oz, $14\frac{1}{2}$ in. pull, $28\frac{1}{4}$ in. barrels, approx. $\frac{1}{2}$ & $\frac{5}{8}$ choke, $2\frac{3}{4}$ in. chambers, nitro proof; cased.

7 Back action guns

Back action guns are, as has been discussed previously, renowned for their strength but they are still seen, rather negatively, as old-fashioned and not of the same quality as a sidelock. The latter is erroneous and Holland & Holland, for example, built very many 'Dominion' actions to a particularly high standard. They remain an undervalued and rather neglected area of the market but I expect the present steadily diminishing supply of best guns to rectify this.

(a) Good to excellent condition: Pairs £3,000 – £5,000, Single £1,500 – £2,500

C. LANCASTER: a 12-bore assisted-opening backlock ejector gun No. 8549; faceted fences, back-action lockplates of leg-of-mutton form, best foliate-scroll engraving, figured stock, lever-latch forend, rebrowned Damascus barrels; weight 6 lb 12 oz, $14\frac{1}{2}$ in. stock, 30 in. barrels, approx. I.C. & $\frac{3}{8}$ choke, $2\frac{1}{2}$ in. chambers, nitro proof.

(b) Average to good condition: Pairs £1,500 – £3,000, Single £800 – £1,500

HOLLAND & HOLLAND: a 12-bore backlock ejector gun No. 26846; 'Grade C', border engraving with some hardening colour, well-figured stock with butt plate; weight 6 lb 11 oz, $13\frac{3}{4}$ in. pull, 30 in. barrels (top rib loose, bores dented and bulged), approx. I.C. & $\frac{5}{8}$ choke, $2\frac{1}{2}$ in. chambers, nitro proof; cased.

(c) Defective/poor to average condition: Pairs £500 – £1,500, Single £250 – £800

HOLLAND & HOLLAND: a 12-bore 'Dominion' backlock non-ejector gun No. 20251; border engraving, well-figured stock with extension; weight 6 lb 14 oz, $13\frac{1}{2}$ in. pull, 30 in. barrels, approx. cyl. & $\frac{1}{2}$ choke, $2\frac{1}{2}$ in. chambers, nitro reproof; cased.

As we have seen, most non-ejector guns are too impractical for modern shooting but they are still of excellent value to beginners. Occasionally a best example of a non-ejector gun will excite keen bidding from a combination of collectors (who will keep the gun as a non-ejector) and dealers/gunsmiths (who will convert is to ejector).

8 Non-ejector guns

Two non-ejector guns: (*left*) a Rigby best quality example, No. 15806 with its Rigby-Bissell rising third-bite and dipped-edge lockplates; (*right*) a Holland & Holland, No. 11220, with border engraving.

(a) Good to excellent condition: Sidelocks £1,500 – £3,500, Boxlocks £300 – £600, Backlocks £500 – £900

J. PURDEY: a 12-bore self-opening sidelock non-ejector gun No. 11346 (1883); the fences chiselled in relief with stylized acanthus leaves, best bouquet and scroll engraving with much hardening colour, highly-figured stock with butt plate, Whitworth steel barrels with game rib; weight 6 lb 10 oz, $14\frac{3}{8}$ in. pull, 30 in. barrels, approx. I.C. & $\frac{1}{2}$ choke, $2\frac{1}{2}$ in. chambers, Black Powder proof (bore-dimensions marginal; right barrel-thickness below recommended minimum); with a set of interchangeable extra 28 in. chopper lump barrels by W. Powell; cased.

LANG & HUSSEY: a 12-bore backlock non-ejector gun No. 13056; best foliate-scroll engraving, brushed bright and reblued finish, well-figured stock with recoil pad, rebrowned Damascus barrels; weight 6 lb $15\frac{1}{2}$ oz, $14\frac{7}{8}$ in. pull, 30 in. barrels, approx. cyl. & $\frac{3}{4}$ choke, $2\frac{1}{2}$ in. chambers, nitro reproof; cased.

(b) Average to good condition: Sidelocks £500 – £1,500, Boxlocks £150 – £350, Backlocks £200 – £500

W.W. GREENER: a 12-bore ($2\frac{3}{4}$ in.) 'Empire' boxlock non-ejector gun No. 78326; manual side safe, border engraving with traces of hardening colour, figured stock with semi-pistolgrip and butt plate, barrels with matt rib; weight 7 lb $12\frac{1}{2}$ oz, $14\frac{3}{8}$ in. pull, 32 in. barrels, both approx. $\frac{7}{8}$ choke, $2\frac{3}{4}$ in. chambers, nitro proof.

ARMY & NAVY: a 12-bore sidelock non-ejector gun No. 58325; foliate-scroll engraving with traces of hardening colour, figured stock with butt plate; weight 6 lb 13 oz, 15 in. pull, 30 in. barrels, approx. cyl. & $\frac{3}{4}$ choke, $2\frac{1}{2}$ in. chambers, nitro proof.

(c) Defective/poor to average condition: Sidelocks £200 – £500, Boxlocks £50 – £150, Backlocks, £100 – £200

COGSWELL & HARRISON: a light 12-bore 'The Desideratum' boxlock non-ejector gun No. 20718; serpentine fences, full foliate-scroll engraving, stock with butt plate; weight 6 lb $4\frac{1}{2}$ oz, $14\frac{7}{8}$ in. pull, 28 in. barrels, both approx. cyl., $2\frac{1}{2}$ in. chambers, nitro proof.

9 Hammer and hammer ejector guns and rifles

There is a new and growing market for hammer guns and the later and more advanced they are, and therefore the better suited to use, the more popular. As in other areas, the better the maker, grade and condition, the higher the price; there is no appreciable likelihood of growth in the market for poor and extensively damaged hammer guns. The term 'proof exemption' indicates that a firearm has been examined at a Proof House, but not proved as either (a) it was deemed of interest and not intended for use, or (b) ammunition was not available.

A .360 (2¼ in. Black Powder) double-barrelled hammer rifle by E.M. Reilly, No. 18748, with a Purdey patent snap action thumb hole underlever. The gun is of particularly high quality.

In either case, the firearm must be regarded as unsafe to fire unless subsequently reproved.

(a) Good to excellent condition: Hammer guns – Pairs £4,000 – £8,000, Single £2,000 – £4,000; Hammer ejector guns – Pairs £8,000 – £15,000; Single £4,000 – £8,000

J. DICKSON: a Charles Gordon 10-bore ($2\frac{7}{8}$ in.) double-barrelled hammer gun No. 4425 (1891); Jones patent rotary underlever, non-rebounding backlocks, percussion fences, best close foliate-scroll engraving with scenes of game birds and gun dogs, boldly-figured stock with butt plate, elongated top and bottom straps, browned Damascus barrels; weight 9 lb 3 oz, $14\frac{5}{8}$ in. pull, 32 in. barrels, approx. cyl. & $\frac{3}{8}$ choke, $2\frac{7}{8}$ in. chambers, nitro reproof.

(b) Average to good condition: Single – £500 – £1,500

WESTLEY RICHARDS: a Westley Richards 1864 patent 12-bore (pin-fire) bar-in-wood hammer gun No. 11457 (1867); patent toplever opening action, the bar-in-wood extending to cover the forend hinge in a 'crab' joint, the sidelocks with dolphin hammers, best foliate-scroll engraving with some hardening colour, figured stock cast off towards central vision, browned Damascus barrels; weight 7 lb, $13\frac{1}{2}$ in. pull, 30 in. barrels, proof exemption.

J. PURDEY: a Purdey 1863 patent hammer gun No. 8021; Second Pattern thumb hole underlever, percussion fences, non-rebounding backlocks, best foliate-scroll engraving, highly-figured stock, sleeved barrels; weight 6 lb 6 oz, $14\frac{1}{4}$ in. pull, $28\frac{1}{8}$ in. barrels, approx. cyl. & $\frac{1}{4}$ choke, $2\frac{1}{2}$ in. chambers, nitro proof; cased.

J. PURDEY: a Bastin-system 12-bore (pin-fire) slide-action hammer gun No. 6746 (1864); Bastin underlever with integral pivoted latch, backlock action with high-spurred dolphin hammers, the hammer noses recessed to receive the car-

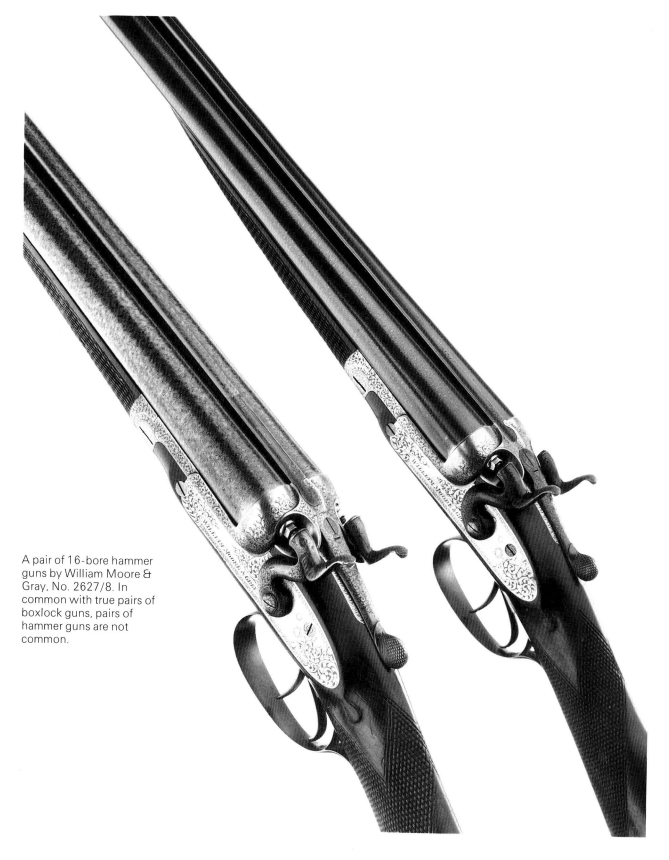

A pair of 16-bore hammer guns by William Moore & Gray, No. 2627/8. In common with true pairs of boxlock guns, pairs of hammer guns are not common.

tridge pins, serpentine fences, best foliate-scroll engraving, figured stock with butt plate, elongated top and bottom straps, browned Damascus barrels; weight 7 lb $\frac{1}{2}$ oz, $14\frac{1}{4}$ in. pull, 30 in. barrels, proof exemption.

(c) Defective/poor to average condition: Single: £100 – £500

W. POWELL: a Powell 1869 patent bar-in-wood hammer gun No. 6663; patent lift-up toplever with patent retracting striker action, rebounding sidelocks, border engraving, the stock with butt plate, rebrowned Damascus barrels; $14\frac{3}{8}$ in. pull, 29 in. barrels, proof exemption, sold as unsuitable for use.

The market for sporting rifles in modern calibres remains very good indeed and there is particular interest in classic double rifles whatever the condition, age or calibre. The combination of a best rifle by one of the most famous makers in one of the most useful big game calibres will generate phenomenal interest. In general, the older and more obsolete the calibre, the less interest but on occasions the rifle will be a focus of attention for collectors and those who will convert it to a more popular calibre.

10   Sporting rifles

(a) Good to excellent condition: £20,000 – £30,000 +

HOLLAND & HOLLAND: a fine Preater-engraved .300 (H. & H. Magnum) '1985 Sesquicentennial Royal de Luxe' d.b. hammerless single trigger sidelock ejector rifle No. 35545 (1985); fully selective single trigger with rolled edge triggerguard, automatic safe, the bolstered treble grip action body with elongated top strap, the lockplates and underside of the action body with de luxe game scene engraving, the triggerplate signed 'K.E. PREATER ENGR.', bright finish overall, highly-figured stock with pistolgrip, cheekpiece and leather-covered recoil pad, sling swivels, the chopper lump barrels with matt sight rib, open sights and ramp-mounted bead foresight with foldaway moon sight, the sight rib mounted with a Leupold Vari-X-III 1.5 X 5 telescope in quickly detachable mounts; weight 10 lb, $14\frac{1}{4}$ in. pull, 24 in. barrels, nitro proof; cased.

HOLLAND & HOLLAND: a fine .375 Magnum (Flanged) 'Royal' d.b. hammerless sidelock ejector rifle No. 28428 (1913); automatic safe, hand-detachable locks, best engraving of bold foliate scrolls with full hardening colour, boldly figured stock with pistolgrip, cheekpiece and recoil pad, the top strap mounted with a folding peepsight, sling eyes, the Whitworth steel chopper lump barrels with matt rear sight block, open sights and ramp-mounted bead foresight with removable hood, the muzzles with matt finish; weight 9 lb 8 oz, $14\frac{1}{2}$ in. pull, 26 in. barrels, nitro proof.

(b) **Average to good condition: £7,000 – £15,000**

J. RIGBY: a .303 d.b. hammerless sidelock ejector rifle No. 17711 (1912); toplever, treble grip action with Rigby-Bissell patent rising third bite, automatic safe with stalking latch, the fences carved with a raised and engraved acanthus leaf motif, dipped edge lockplates, best engraving of bold foliate scrolls with some hardening colour, well-figured stock with pistolgrip, cheekpiece and engraved iron butt plate, sling swivel and bolt, lever latch forend, chopper lump barrels with matt sight rib, open sights and ramp-mounted bead foresight; weight 8 lb 15½ oz, 14⅞ in. pull, 26 in. barrels, nitro proof; cased.

HOLLAND & HOLLAND: a fine .240 (Flanged) 'Royal' d.b. hammerless back-lock ejector rifle No. 28461 (1919); Holland & Holland patent treble grip action with side bolsters and elongated top strap, bolted automatic safe, best bold engraving of foliate scrollwork with some hardening colour, boldly figured stock with pistolgrip and butt plate, the chopper lump barrels with matt rear sight block, open sights and ramp-mounted bead foresight; weight 8 lb 6 oz, 14⅝ in. pull, 25 in. barrels, nitro proof; cased.

(c) **Defective/poor to average condition: £2,000 – £7,000**

J. WOODWARD: a .303 'The Automatic' d.b. hammerless sidelock non-ejector rifle No. 5383 (*circa* 1900); snap action underlever, treble grip action with side

A fine and ornate single-barrelled target rifle by T. Laüger of Lörrach, the stock inset with a silver presentation plaque bearing the inscription, 'Presented in July 1861, on the occasion of the German Marksmen's Day in Gotha, to the assembled members of the Guild of Marksmen of Frankfurt on Oder'. The full complement of accessories also includes the winning target.

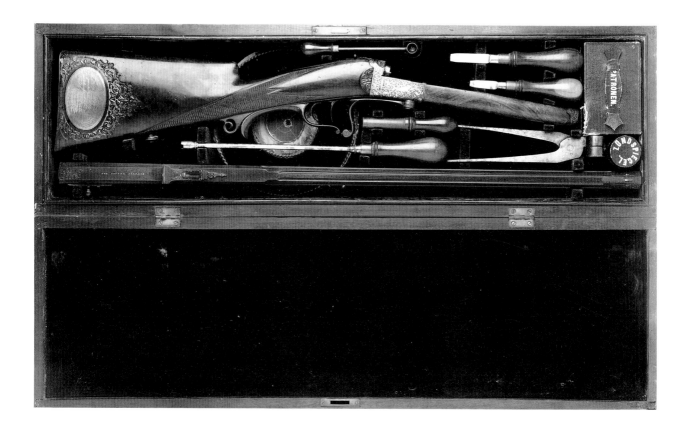

clips and flat elongated breech flat, bolted automatic safe, protruding tumbler pivots, arcaded fences, best foliate-scroll engraving with traces of hardening colour, well-figured stock with pistolgrip, cheekpiece and recoil pad, sling bolts, Whitworth steel chopper lump barrels with matt rib, open sights and ramp-mounted bead foresight; weight 9 lb 4 oz, $14\frac{3}{4}$ in. pull, 28 in. barrels, nitro proof; cased.

HOLLAND & HOLLAND: a .22 (Hornet) d.b. hammerless 'Royal' sidelock non-ejector rifle No. 28417; converted from .360 calibre, hand-detachable locks, rounded bar, automatic safe (bolted safety lever removed), elongated top strap, best bold engraving of foliate scrollwork, stock with pistolgrip, cheekpiece and recoil pad, Whitworth steel chopper lump barrels with open sights and ramp-mounted bead foresight, the matt sight rib with telescope shoes; weight 8 lb $15\frac{1}{2}$ oz, $13\frac{1}{2}$ in. pull, 26 in. barrels, nitro proof.

Boxlock ejector & non-ejector

(a) **Good to excellent condition:** £4,000 – £8,000

(b) **Average to good condition:** £1,500 – £4,000

(c) **Defective/poor to average condition:** £500 – £1,500

W. EVANS: a .470 ($3\frac{1}{4}$ in. Nitro Express) d.b. hammerless boxlock ejector rifle No. 14356; automatic safe, full foliate-scroll engraving, brushed bright and reblued finish, figured stock with pistolgrip and recoil pad (replacement forend wood), sling eyes, the chopper lump barrels with matt sight rib, open sights and ramp-mounted bead foresight with folding moonsight; weight 10 lb 14 oz, $14\frac{3}{4}$ in. pull, 26 in. barrels, nitro proof; cased.

W.J. JEFFERY: a .450/.400 (3in. Nitro Express) d.b. hammerless boxlock non-ejector rifle No. 15396; manual safe, plain finish, the sides of the action bar engraved with scenes of Cape Buffalo, figured stock with pistolgrip and recoil pad, sling eyes, the Krupp-steel chopper lump barrels with matt top rib, open sights and ramp-mounted bead foresight; weight 10 lb 10 oz, $15\frac{1}{4}$ in. pull, 24 in. barrels, nitro proof; cased.

Mauser: Magnum action £1,500 – £5,500 + ; Standard Action £500 – £1,500

Mannlicher Schoenauer: £200 – £500

Falling block: £1,000 – £6,000 +

Rook rifles: £200 – £600

A selection of shooting accessories and curiosities including two very unusual Irvine gun-lock testers for 12 and 20-bore. The selection also includes a pewter priming powder flask, a game counter, a Victorian wooden paperweight carved with 'Spoils of the Chase' and a miniature cannon barrel.

11 Accessories

As with the later rifle sections, this section will be dealt with more generally and it is important to note that accessories are rarely encountered in anything other than used or average to poor condition. Those encountered in excellent condition will understandably bring a premium.

Guncases (for classic barrel lengths: 27, 28, 29, 30 in.)
Brass mounted double oak and leather: £200 – £600 +
Brass mounted single oak and leather: £100 – £400
Double leather: £200 – £400
Single leather: £100 – £300
Brass mounted oak and leather triple: £200 – £600 +

Cartridge magazines (in varying sizes – 150, 200, 250 and 400 capacity etc.)
Brass mounted oak and leather: £200 – £600 +

Place finders
Asprey's: £500 – £1,500 +
'Norfolk Liars': £200 – £500

Cartridge boards
Classic Eley configuration: £1,000 – £2,500

Cartridge mirrors
Classic Eley configuration: £200 – £500

'Gannochy' cartridge dispensers:
£200 – £500

Leather cartridge bags: £50 – £150

Leg-of-mutton cases: £50 – £150

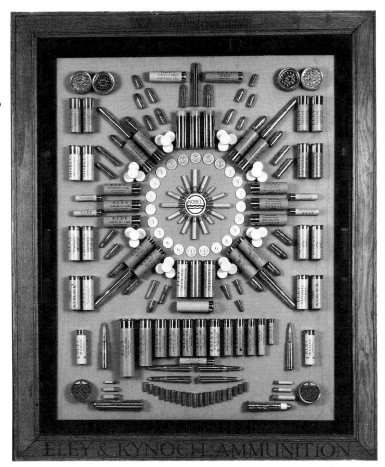

A cartridge board.

Rarities and 'special' guns of the following types have achieved the prices shown for their inherent qualities; 'condition', whilst being of enormous benefit, is a somewhat less important factor here.

12 Unusual guns

J. PURDEY: a fine pair of 12-bore ($2\frac{3}{4}$ in.) self-opening sidelock ejector game guns No. 28152/3 (1973–1977); profusely gold encrusted by K.C. Hunt. £121,000 (1989).

J. PURDEY: a fine pair of 12-bore ($2\frac{3}{4}$ in.) single trigger under-and-over sidelock ejector game guns No. 28275/6 (1976–1983); profusely gold encrusted and gold-damascened by K.C. Hunt. $187,000 (1988).

BOSS: a .410 (3 in.) single trigger over-and-under sidelock ejector game gun No. 8619 (1938); the first .410 over-and-under gun to have been built by this maker. $112,000 (1989)

BOSS: a 28-bore over-and-under sidelock ejector game gun No. 7254 (1925). £47,700 (1974).

J. DICKSON: a Dickson & Murray 1882 patent three barrel, two trigger 16-bore round action ejector gun No. 4801 (1896). Value possibly in excess of £50,000.

BOSS over-and-under double rifles: No known examples at auction. Value possibly in excess of £50,000.

J. DICKSON: Charles Gordon's 4-bore (4 in.) double-barrelled hammer gun No. 4234 (1888). £17,600 (1993).

J. PURDEY: Lord Ripon's 12-bore hammer gun No. 10886 (1881). £8,050 (1993).

Large bore wildfowling pieces, including punt guns: Punt guns £500 – £2,500 +. Wildfowling guns £500 – £5,000 (depending upon bore size and configuration).

A 1½ in. Bland-Nordenfelt single-barrelled breech loading punt gun by T. Bland. A rare example, the design was praised for the practicality of the one piece construction of its nickel steel barrel and action body, the curtailment of recoil (about 2 in. with a full load) and the low mounting permitted by its breech and extractor systems.

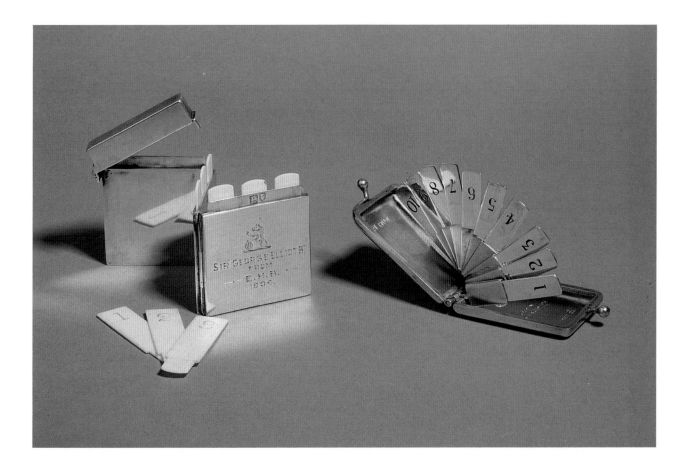

PLATE 23 *(above)* An unusual Asprey's silver place finder, the small lidded tablet unfolding in three hinged sections to present the numbered markers and dating from 1904; and a silver 'Patent Pathfinder' by G. White & Co. (1911). Items such as these are amongst the most prized of sporting gun accessories. *(below)* The engraved and gold-washed lock work of Holland & Holland sidelock, No. 40224.

PLATE 24   A fine Eley 'Sporting and Military' cartridge board.

Small bore guns of various types

Small bore guns have become particularly desirable in recent years. The following are a selection of some of the most desirable types.

J. PURDEY: a pair of .410 (3 in.) self-opening sidelock ejector guns No. 28323/4 (1980); unused; each gun with a set of interchangeable extra barrels. £37,400 (1991).

J. PURDEY: a set of three 28-bore ($2\frac{3}{4}$ in.) self-opening sidelock ejector guns No. 28207/8/9 (1977); unused. £55,000 (1991).

BOSS: a pair of 20-bore ($2\frac{3}{4}$ in.) single trigger sidelock ejector guns No. 7313/4 (1926); standard easy opening action, Boss patent single triggers with rolled edge triggerguards, best bouquet and scroll engraving with much hardening colour, well-figured stocks, Whitworth steel chopper lump barrels with game ribs; weight 5 lb 10 oz (No. 1) and 5 lb 9 oz (No. 2), $14\frac{3}{8}$ in. stocks, 28 in. barrels, all approx. $\frac{1}{4}$ choke, $2\frac{3}{4}$ in. chambers, nitro reproof (No. 2 left barrel thickness marginal); cased. £38,500 (1991).

J. PURDEY: a 20-bore self-opening sidelock ejector gun No. 16663 (1899); the fences chiselled in relief with stylized acanthus leaves, best bouquet and scroll engraving with much hardening colour, highly-figured stock with engraved plates at the toe and heel, Whitworth steel chopper lump barrels with game rib; weight 5 lb 13 oz, $14\frac{1}{2}$ in. stock, 29 in. barrels, approx. I.C. & $\frac{3}{4}$ choke, $2\frac{1}{2}$ in. chambers; cased. £14,300 (1991).

W. POWELL: a 28-bore boxlock ejector gun No. 197; scroll-back action body, the fences relief engraved with foliage and flowers, best bouquet and scroll engraving with much hardening colour, well-figured stock, the barrels with matt Churchill-style rib; weight 5 lb $5\frac{1}{2}$ oz, $14\frac{3}{8}$ in. stock, 27 in. barrels, approx. $\frac{1}{4}$ and $\frac{3}{8}$ choke, $2\frac{1}{2}$ in. chambers, nitro proof; cased. £1,540 (1992).

WATSON: a .410 boxlock ejector gun No. 7000; best bold foliate-scroll engraving with much hardening colour, highly-figured stock with semi-pistolgrip and butt plate; weight 4 lb $4\frac{1}{2}$ oz, $13\frac{7}{8}$ in. pull, 27 in. barrels, both approx. $\frac{1}{4}$ choke, $2\frac{1}{2}$ in. chambers, nitro reproof; cased. £1,760 (1992).

ENGRAVING

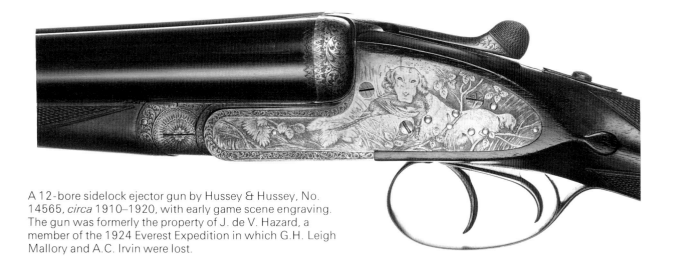

A 12-bore sidelock ejector gun by Hussey & Hussey, No. 14565, *circa* 1910–1920, with early game scene engraving. The gun was formerly the property of J. de V. Hazard, a member of the 1924 Everest Expedition in which G.H. Leigh Mallory and A.C. Irvin were lost.

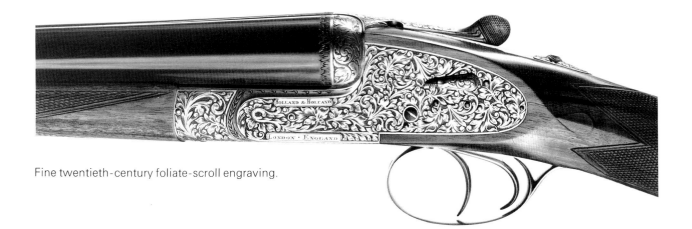

Fine twentieth-century foliate-scroll engraving.

The Greener 'St George' Show Gun,
No. 52227, completed *circa* 1903.

Game engraving on a pair of 12-bore (2¾ in.) 'Royal de Luxe' self-opening sidelock ejector guns by Holland & Holland, No. 40133/4. The guns were completed *circa* 1974 and were engraved by Ken Hunt with scenes of teal, red-leg partridge, pheasant, grey partridge, red grouse and mallard. Note the hand-detachable levers and the rolled edge trigger guards.

(*This page and opposite*) A fine pair of 12-bore (2¾ in.) sidelock ejector guns by
J. Roberts, No. 2235/6 with de luxe engraving by Ken Hunt. The guns were completed
circa 1979 and were embellished with scenes taken from the heroic fantasy of Conan the
Barbarian.

A selection of twentieth-century engraving styles.

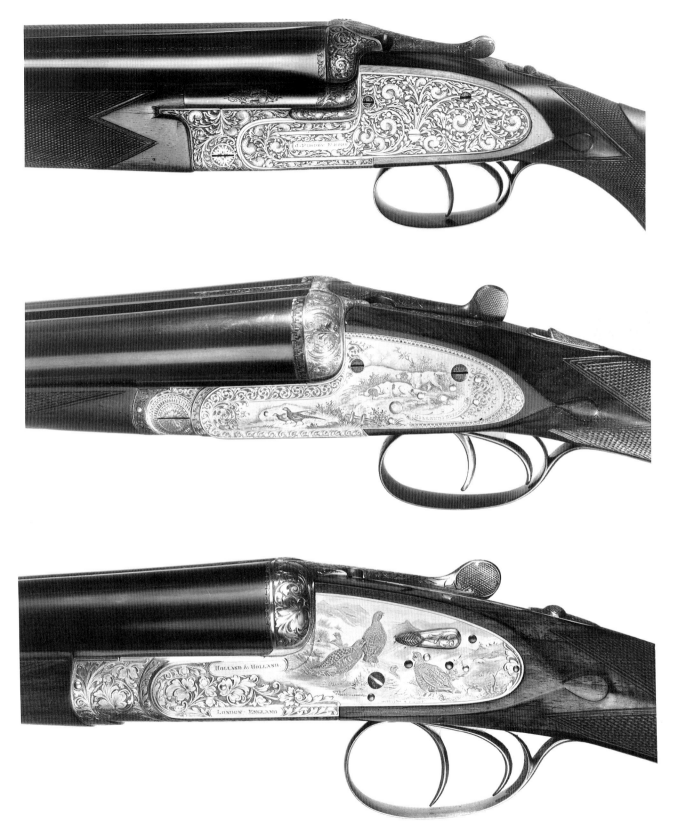

INDEX

Italics refer to black and white illustrations